Anywhere, USA

A Memoir

Steph Silver

Sulit Press

Paperback: 979-8-9880332-2-6

Ebook: 979-8-9880332-3-3

Edited by Erin Althaus

Cover art by Christy Jaynes

Sulit Press

www.sulitpress.com

Dedication

This book is dedicated to my friends, family, and everyone who has provided a helping hand, a smile, or a bit of confidence along the way. If your name is left out of these pages, it's not because you are forgotten. You definitely have a place in my heart, and you may have a cameo in the made-for-TV series; there just aren't enough pages to tell every story.

Special thanks goes to Michelle and Bobbie. You are my only tether other than God to consistent and unconditional love.

I want it to be known from beginning to end that I found light, laughter, and happiness in almost every experience and now find gratitude for all of them.

Contents

Introduction   VII

Moving Timeline   X

Chapter 1   1

Chapter 2   5

Chapter 3   23

Chapter 4   31

Chapter 5   38

Chapter 6   47

Chapter 7   59

Chapter 8   68

Chapter 9   78

Chapter 10   86

Chapter 11   94

Chapter 12   103

Chapter 13   110

Chapter 14   116

Chapter 15 128

Chapter 16 136

Chapter 17 146

Chapter 18 159

Chapter 19 170

Chapter 20 184

Acknowledgments 194

Introduction

B eginning this book at the beginning of my life feels unimaginative. Unlike memoirs that highlight one's achievements in adulthood and work their way backward, my story begins with what happened to me before I have a clear memory of my own. From a time when few photographs exist, I'm left with dreamlike snapshots tucked into the ripples of my mind that spring forth at unpredictable intervals.

There are the stories that people in my life told me about me before I could remember things for myself. Then there are the things I remember as reliably as anyone can remember anything. And finally, in a collaborative effort to piece together the complex cartography of what happened where and when, my siblings and family friends have spent hours puzzling together a forensic account of the truth, however elusive it may feel.

Even when we agree on the events, the locations, and the timeline in which things occurred, our individual experiences are vastly different. For this reason, I'm aware this book is dishonest by default; however, every word of it is *my* truth.

By the time I graduated from high school, I had lived in more than thirty places, though I can't say I'd call all of them homes. Two weeks here, three months there, our family moved at the whim of my father, who changed his mind like winds in a winter storm. Frequently, sporadically, and often without warning, we'd pack only what could fit into the car and go.

The question I get asked most when telling someone about my life is, "Why?" Why in the world did you move from a comfortable, four-bedroom house on a lake to a campground? Why did you attend five schools in eighth grade? Why did your parents spend most of their money on booze and pot and cigarettes when they had so little to spare? And most importantly, why didn't you leave when you had the chance?

'Why' is the question I've asked myself a million times and will never be able to answer. But 'how' is the question I'm answering now. How did I survive my circumstances? How did I know there was always love present in the midst of so much chaos? How did I pull my life together instead of becoming a statistic? And how do I know that no matter how hard or sad or totally fucked up life might feel, light is also present?

The origin stories I usually find most intriguing retrace the events that led to someone becoming something remarkable or unusual, like the president, an Olympic athlete, or a serial killer. Few people look at a middle-aged white mom and think, *Man! I sure wish I knew how that white lady with a good job and a giant house in the suburbs got her start in life!* But considering where my life began, the fact I "pass" as a regular suburban mom is one of the most remarkable things I can imagine.

My story isn't just about arriving at a station in life that, while ordinary to many Americans, was nowhere on my radar as a child. It's about surviving a number of close calls with death and "sliding door" moments where even the smallest change in circumstances could have sent me careening into a totally different life or ended it altogether. Whether saved by a kind shop owner, guardian angels, the police, or an occasional block of (truly delicious) government cheese, I reflect with gratitude for the grace that's gotten me this far.

Lastly, I should mention the story you're about to read may leave you scratching your head, and you'll likely need to refer back to the timeline to keep up. It's like one of those Scandinavian novels where everyone is named Born and Thorn and Yorn, which were also the names of their sons and fathers and grandfathers. Fortunately, everyone in my family bears a unique name of their own (although I've changed a few for privacy reasons), so instead of including a family tree, I've included a timeline of all the places I've lived. Feel free to dog-ear the page for easy referral. (Unless this is a library book, then you should use a bookmark like a good and respectful citizen.)

MOVING TIMELINE
1980-2022

- 1980 - BORN IN SAPULPA, OKLAHOMA (NEAR TULSA)
- 1982 - KIDNAPPING (OREGON)
- 1982 - WAGONER, OKLAHOMA
- 1982 - TULSA, OKLAHOMA - RANCH
- 1982 - LAKE TAHOE, CALIFORNIA - ROADSIDE
- 1982 - CALIFORNIA SHELTERS
- 1982 - STANDISH-HICKEY CAMPGROUND, CALIFORNIA
- 1983 - COLORADO - SHELTER
- 1983 - BOULDER, COLORADO - APARTMENT
- 1983 - SCOTTSDALE, ARIZONA
- 1983 - STANDISH-HICKEY CAMPGROUND, CALIFORNIA
- 1983 - KELLY'S CAMPGROUND, CALIFORNIA
- 1984 - GUERNEVILLE, CALIFORNIA
- 1984 - SANTA ROSA, CALIFORNIA
- 1984 - CLEARLAKE OAKS, CALIFORNIA
- 1985 - CARSON CITY, NEVADA
- 1986 - VIRGINIA CITY, NEVADA - GREEN HOUSE ON K STREET
- 1987 - TULSA, OKLAHOMA - HOUSE 1
- 1987 - TULSA, OKLAHOMA - HOUSE 2
- 1988 - BOULDER CITY, NEVADA
- 1988 - VIRGINIA CITY, NEVADA - STUDIO ABOVE RED'S CANDIES
- 1988 - DAVIS CREEK CAMPGROUND, NEVADA
- 1988 - RENO, NEVADA - EL PATIO MOTEL (NOT MENTIONED)
- 1989 - VIRGINIA CITY, NEVADA - SUGARLOAF MOTEL (NOT MENTIONED)
- 1990 - VIRGINIA CITY, NEVADA - HOUSE ON CARSON STREET
- 1992 - VIRGINIA CITY, NEVADA - RED HOUSE ON L STREET
- 1992 - VIRGINIA CITY, NEVADA - WHITE HOUSE ON L STREET
- 1992 - CAMPGROUNDS ACROSS THE WEST
- 1992 - ST. GEORGE, UTAH - CAMPGROUND
- 1992 - ST. GEORGE, UTAH - MOTEL
- 1992 - MESQUITE, NEVADA - MOTEL

- 1992 – UKIAH, CALIFORNIA – SHELTER
- 1992/93 – UKIAH, CALIFORNIA
- 1993 – CARSON CITY, NEVADA
- 1993 – EVANSTON, WYOMING – HOTEL
- 1993 – CARSON CITY, NEVADA
- 1993 – INOLA, OKLAHOMA
- 1993/94 – MESQUITE, NEVADA
- 1994 – MINERAL WELLS, TEXAS
- 1994 – GRAFORD, TEXAS
- 1996/97 – WAGONER, OKLAHOMA
- 1997/98 – GRAFORD, TEXAS
- 1998 – VIRGINIA CITY, NEVADA
- 1998 – STEPHENVILLE, TEXAS – TARLETON DORM, FRESHMAN YEAR
- 1999 – GRAFORD, TEXAS
- 1999 – STEPHENVILLE, TEXAS – TARLETON DORM & RITA'S APARTMENT, SOPHOMORE YEAR
- 2000 – GULF SHORES, ALABAMA
- 2000 – TAYLOR, TEXAS
- 2000 – AUSTIN, TEXAS – METROPOLIS APARTMENTS
- 2001 – AUSTIN, TEXAS – NORTH AUSTIN
- 2002 – SAN MARCOS, TEXAS
- 2002 – AUSTIN, TEXAS – NORTH AUSTIN, MATTHEW'S APARTMENT
- 2003 – AUSTIN, TEXAS – MENCHACA 4-PLEX
- 2004 – AUSTIN, TEXAS – APARTMENT ON S 1ST
- 2005 – AUSTIN, TEXAS – BRIAR RIDGE, PURCHASED 1ST HOME
- 2015 – DRIFTWOOD, TEXAS
- 2017 – GRANDMA DIED IN HER HOME IN OKLAHOMA
- 2018 – MOM DIED IN GEORGETOWN, TEXAS
- 2019 – DAD DIED IN ROUND ROCK, TEXAS
- 2021 – MOM'S ASHES IN VIRGINIA CITY, NEVADA
- 2021 – KYLE, TEXAS – DIVORCE
- 2022 – WIMBERLEY, TEXAS

Chapter 1

I've seen more of this country than most people but not the places people want to see. The first time I remember riding cross-country in the back of a car, I was very young, just two years old. My small body strapped tightly to the red leather seat inside a red car, I cried most of the way between Oklahoma and Oregon. The driver did little to comfort me, which is an odd way for a father to behave, but it was perhaps in alignment with his new role as my kidnapper. I wasn't crying because I feared my father or because I had any understanding that I might not see my mom and siblings again. I wasn't old enough to know that. I only knew I was being separated without explanation and that I'd left without my brother, and that just wasn't a thing that ever happened. Bobbie and I were always very tight and always together as confidants and playmates. I was scared because I was alone.

It wasn't a mystery who I was with, only where he was taking me and what would happen to me after that. Stephen Mallory, my biological father, was a known pedophile even before my mother married him. She'd been warned by one of his sisters and other women in his family that he was not to be trusted around children, especially girls. But he treated her better than anyone else had before and made her feel so good about herself that she pushed away any thoughts or talk of the terrible things that he had done.

Pat, short for Patricia, was already pregnant with me when she married Stephen. This was my mother's second marriage. Her first was to her high school sweetheart, with whom she thought she was in love but was still too young to know for sure. By the time Mom and Stephen met at a junior college in Muskogee, she'd already had my older siblings, Michelle and Bobbie, who were three years apart. The exact timeline is unclear as to whether my mom had officially divorced her first husband before getting together with Stephen, but with me on the way, it probably moved things along.

Bobbie is two years older than me, and Michelle is five years older, so between having two small children and a baby on the way, Mom and Stephen had a full house from the start. Stephen also had another daughter my sister's age named Decenda, but I've never met her.

Photos of me as a baby calmly snuggled on Stephen's chest look the same as any other newborn-daddy photos. He looked tender and gentle, and for the most part, he was. Then again, being kind to kids to win their trust sort of goes with the territory of being a pedophile. What exactly happened to my siblings behind closed doors and how my mother turned a blind eye are questions I can't answer. I wonder where the tipping point is between being a proud father and becoming a predator.

Mom had only been married to Stephen for about a year and a half when she left him to be with Byron. I'd like to think that she left Stephen because of things that were happening in her house when he was alone with the kids, but if Byron hadn't been a soft place to land, she probably would have stayed. Raising three kids alone on a waitress salary was scarier to her than either living with a pedophile or a man she'd just met.

Out of the frying pan into the fire, Byron, for all his wonderful qualities, was a raging alcoholic. And when I say raging, I don't just mean he drank heavily; he also had a volatile temper that exploded at frequent and random intervals. Still, as the lesser of two evils, he was preferable to a pedophile.

Although Mom had already left Stephen for Byron, they were still legally married, which is why the day care I disappeared from did not stop him from taking me, and the police couldn't command him to give me back. With no divorce decree outlining a new custody agreement, Stephen had every legal right to be with me. One day, Mom came to pick up me and Bobbie, but I wasn't there. The day care administrators believed that my dad had picked me up, but Mom called around, and nobody had seen him.

Panicking and distraught, Mom had absolutely no clue where Stephen had taken me. Stephen had several sisters, most of whom protected him. She called the one sister who had warned her about his pedophilia, and she told my mom there was one sister in Oregon who would definitely harbor him, and while she didn't know if he was there, that's where she would look. At that time, we were all living in Tulsa, Oklahoma. My mother couldn't afford to take care of herself and her three kids, much less travel to Oregon on a whim that I might be there. But what choice did she have? It was her only lead. Leaving Michelle and Bobbie with my grandmother, Mom pooled enough money together from aunts and uncles to get a plane ticket to Oregon.

As soon as Mom's plane touched down, she went directly to the police station, where they repeated the same answers the Oklahoma police had given, saying, "We don't have a way of telling where she is, and we have no legal right to take her from her father if we do find her. Since we don't know if he's dangerous or not to the child or to you, we can give you a police escort, but there's nothing else that we can do. The other thing to know is if you go to this woman's house, and he just happens to be out, she will tell him, and he will flee somewhere else. You have no other leads, so this may be your one and only opportunity."

The only thing I can recall from that time, other than the red leather seats in the little red car, is curling up alone under a desk in a hotel room and crying. I don't remember meeting the aunt who'd helped my father hide me or the police knocking on the door to find me, just as I don't remember running into my mother's arms at the one singular moment when I was saved from a life of unknown perils.

What would have become of me if I'd stayed with my father? Would the memories I now struggle to recall be those of my mother's face and a bond with a brother I could barely remember? Knowing what I know now about the hardships in my life that followed, life with Stephen would have been more miserable than the one I've led, but by how much, I cannot measure. In truth, my rescue simply pulled me from one frying pan into another, which makes the concept of being "saved" a relative one.

Chapter 2

From where I sit now, I see there's a natural rhythm to things — not a predictable pattern over which we have any control, but a natural changing of the seasons. Or maybe it's more like breathing — a repetitive cycle of expansion and contraction, a great inhalation followed by a dramatic sigh because what goes up must come down and vice versa. This is to say that after my kidnapping, my family had some time to rest and reset before the next storm.

For about a month, my mom, siblings, and I stayed with Grandma Rhodes, my mom's mom, which provided us with a moment of stability. Grandma Rhodes was the quintessential grandma. She cooked from memory and taste, and while she never used recipes, everything she made was comforting and delicious, including biscuits and gravy and fried pies. She had a huge garden in her backyard and a swing set for dozens of grandkids to play on. She knitted, crocheted, and made quilts for every child and blankets for every baby. We went to church with her on Sundays and spent time with our cousins, aunts, and uncles.

Aside from the snapshot memories from my kidnapping, I only have two other vivid memories from around this time. The first is of walking through a field of beautiful flowers with Bobbie. Mesmerized by the sea of tender petals, I stepped slowly and deliberately, recognizing that something so delicate and vulnerable was worth protecting. I just had to move slowly, be careful, and pay attention.

The third thing I can remember is meeting Byron.

By default, and for obvious reasons, the number of children who remember meeting their parents for the first time is relatively low compared with those who don't, but I'll never forget the first time I met Byron. (I'll refer to Byron as my dad for the rest of this book and for the rest of my life.) When we arrived at his trailer, Byron was sitting on his second-hand sofa, and when he held his hands out to me, I went right to him. We instantly connected. A six-foot-five-inch giant, he was tall and strong with a deep, gravelly voice, dark mustache, wide smile, and beautiful but terrifying blue eyes that somehow still pierced through his Buddy Holly coke bottle glasses. His big hands, made rough from work as a carpet installer, held me while we watched whatever was on TV.

From the start, Byron was as committed to being my father as if he'd made me himself. I was 100 percent a daddy's girl, completely enamored by his awesome smile but still terrified of his explosive temper that was frequently ignited by alcohol. He'd go from cuddling and joking around to screaming, yelling, and pointing in my face in a matter of seconds, without warning. It's tricky being loved by someone who's broken.

I was not, however, the first daughter Byron loved. He'd been married twice before my mom — first to Elsie, who he'd met in high school in Claremore, Oklahoma. He loved Elsie deeply, and after they got married, they had a beautiful little girl named Victoria, Vicki for short. I can only imagine that Vicki had also been a daddy's girl, walking in his shadow, holding his rough hands, and sitting on his lap to watch whatever was on TV.

What a thrill it probably was for Vicki, riding around in the back of her dad's truck, bouncing over gravel roads while he blared country music through open windows, laughing and yelling, "Faster, Daddy, faster!" Or maybe it was nothing like that. Maybe Byron was just headed out to pick up some cigarettes and begrudgingly let her tag along. What Byron couldn't have seen coming was the storm rolling in that would turn his life upside down.

When Vicki was just four years old, she fell out of the back of Byron's truck and suffered extensive brain damage. From that point forward, she had seizures, and her mental capacity diminished to the point where she'd require live-in care for the rest of her life. The emotional pain from Vicki's accident destroyed Byron and Elsie's marriage. While Byron had already been an alcoholic, he needed more than booze to help him forget his pain, so he moved to Colorado, leaving both Elsie and Vicki behind. Elsie remarried, and Vicki moved in with Elsie's parents in Claremore, where they continued to care for her. I didn't know about Vicki until I was seven years old, and while she was in and out of our lives, she was never part of our family.

By the time Mom and Byron got together, he'd already had a second failed marriage and had drunk enough alcohol to fill an Olympic swimming pool, but he did his best to make us into a family. Leaving Grandma Rhodes' house to move in with Byron, we ended up in an old ranch house outside of Tulsa. Just like you might picture, there were about five wide steps that led to a wrap-around porch before you got to the front door. It wasn't a dreamy Scarlett O'Hara-style ranch; it was more like something you'd see in a Chainsaw Massacre remake, but it was a fun place to live.

Around the back of the house were areas where a rabbit may have been caged, and some chickens had cooped many years before. We didn't have any ranch animals, but Bobbie and I pretended to have pigs, chickens, and all the other farm friends we could imagine. There was a huge field next to us that contained an incredibly large black bull. It was made clear to us that we were not to cross the fence to visit the bull because his kick could kill us. Naturally, being told not to do something created a temptation too great for us to bear. Bobbie and I crossed under the barbed wire fence a few times, but even the twitch of the bull's ear would send us running back to safety, full of pure terror and delight.

We did have a few other animals in and around the house, though not by choice. Being in the country, people would abandon their dogs and cats nearby, and they would find their way to our front porch. Though Michelle, Bobbie, and I wanted to keep them, Dad would load them into his truck and take them to someone else's neighborhood. That worked for all but one dog, who found his way back to the house before Dad did. After the fourth return of that dog, we figured he must be ours, so he was allowed to stay. We also had critters that weren't all that welcome, like the field mice we'd chase around the house and the frogs that ended up in our bathtub. Bobbie was terrified of taking baths for years because of those frogs.

The ranch wasn't fancy, but it was sort of an idyllic place for a kid to play and grow up. We could have stayed forever and gone to school there and graduated and married our own high school sweethearts, just like our parents had done, but our path was not going to be such a linear one. For no reason at all and with zero planning or forethought, we left that house one day and never returned. All five of us loaded into the car, leaving everything behind, including the dog, and drove to California. When you're young, you don't have a set expectation of what constitutes a "normal" life, so discarding your house and belongings to sleep in a car on the side of the road wasn't as traumatic for me at three as it probably was for Michelle, who was eight. Mom and Dad looked at everything as an adventure, so I did too.

I don't remember much of the three-day road trip other than sleeping on the floorboard of the car. When we finally pulled off the highway onto a dirt road somewhere near Lake Tahoe, we were all anxious to get out of the car. It had been raining buckets since about the time we crossed into the Golden State, but since we had no place to go, we spent a couple of days sitting in the car on the side of the road, just waiting it out. Dad said we'd get out of the car and look around after it stopped raining, and while we explored, he'd go look for a job. Looking out the windows of the car through the rain, we could see a blur of tall green trees but not much else. I'd been excited about going to a place called the Golden State, but so far, I was unimpressed.

When the sun broke through the clouds, we all climbed out and stretched, and as Dad pulled away, we explored the green paradise. My eyes widened as we walked further up the muddy road and discovered a trail into the trees. It seemed like all the birds and butterflies in this Golden State were just as happy as we were that the rain had stopped. They were all there to greet us and sing to us as we gazed up at the tallest trees in the universe. As we walked further up the trail, we discovered a creek with crystal blue water flowing out of the mountain. That's when Bobbie and I knew that this must be a magical place. We played up there for hours, looking for tadpoles in the water, chasing squirrels, and singing with the birds. The air was crisp and clean in our lungs as we ran around, laughing and getting our energy out.

Eventually, Mom found us and brought us back to the car. Dad had returned from job hunting, and we needed to run some errands. We drove through the winding roads with cliffs on either side, and I couldn't take my eyes off the landscape. It was as if we were driving right through the earth. Dad said we had driven this same road before but that we just couldn't see the cliffs and trees because it had been raining so hard. Just then, Mom said, "SHIT!" and Dad shouted, "Fuck!" Mom yelled out, "Pull over, pull over." "What the fuck do you think I'm doing?" Dad said as he slowed and pulled to the side. Shocked and confused, Michelle, Bobbie, and I all began to pepper them with questions. "What happened? What's going on? Did we pop a tire?" "No," Dad said, with a huge smile on his face. "Your mom's damn underwear is all over the highway." Then he burst into laughter. We all turned around and saw for ourselves that the highway was covered with clothes: one of the suitcases strapped to the top of the car had come open. Mom ran into the road to gather her stuff. "Get your ass back here. Are you fucking stupid? Are you trying to kill yourself? There are too many cars and too many curves. You'll just have to get some new fucking panties. Hopefully, no one gets one of those fucking parachutes on their windshield and flies off the cliff."

Mom was mortified. She picked up what she could from the side of the road and put it back into one of the suitcases. Then she got back in, slumped her head, and began to cry. "What are we going to do? We don't have money to buy new clothes."

As we began to drive away, all three of us were turned backward in our seats, watching the cotton blow in the breeze, getting run over by cars, stuck to the front of large trucks, twisted, and flung back down to the road. "Was any of that ours?" we asked. "Did we lose any of our toys? We'll go get it if you're too scared."

By this time, Dad was laughing hysterically, though frustrated by the constant chatter in the back. "No, just all your mom's parachute panties. Now that's a story we won't forget...when Mom lost her parachute fucking panties on Highway 101." Everyone laughed except Mom, who smacked Dad on the arm and gave him a nasty look.

Arriving in town, though I'm not sure which town it was, we pulled up to a big building and went in. Everyone was kind, and there were small boxes in each corner with toys. Mom and Dad told us to be very quiet while they talked with the people behind the desk. I could hear them talking about a home, and I figured we must be buying one — how exciting! I hoped that maybe we could take some of these fun toys with us to our new house because we didn't have much in our car.

After we left that office, we drove down the street to another big building. This time, Mom went in by herself. We sat in the warm car for a couple of hours, frequently asking when we could get out, when Mom was coming back, if we could go in with her, and a hundred other pestering questions. Dad drove around the block a few times to try to entertain us but said that wasted too much gas. Eventually, Mom walked out and joined us in the car. She rubbed her arm and gave Dad an envelope. She said she didn't get as much money as she had hoped but that it would help. Mom tried to avoid the questions about what she was doing and why it took so long, but we were pretty persistent, so she finally relented and told us she had just donated plasma for money. She said they don't give money for just blood anymore, so she had to stay a little longer and let them take her plasma. This only encouraged another set of inquiries from us, but tired and frustrated, she answered as much as she could before telling us to be quiet.

We went to the dollar store, then the liquor store, and then headed back up the mountain. I asked Mom when we were going to get a house, and she said we'd have to check back tomorrow. That got me super excited.

At the dollar store, Mom bought some food, replenished a few of the clothes that had escaped from her suitcase, and found some candy, toys, and eggs for our Easter baskets. Apparently, it was Easter, and we had all forgotten.

When we got back to our spot up the dirt road, Bobbie, Michelle, and I all popped out of the car and began to hide and search for the eggs. That kept us entertained until the sun went down, and then we piled back into the car for another night. Dad slept in the driver's seat, Mom in the passenger's seat, Michelle in the back seat, and Bobbie and I tucked nicely into the back floorboards. I remember feeling cozy and safe there with all of us together.

In the morning, we drove back to town — we could see Mom's clothes still strung up and down the highway, and we all joked about the parachute panties. I asked if they could really be used as a parachute if someone wanted to jump from one of those tall cliffs. Clearly unamused, Mom sharply said, "NO!"

After stopping for a moment at the same office we all went to the day before, we drove a bit further and parked at a house. Inside, there was a tall staircase to the right, a really nice living room with a television in the middle, and a clean kitchen with a large table to the left. A very nice woman showed us around all the public areas and then walked us up the stairs to the rooms. I thought it was super cool that I could see into the kitchen and living room and watch the other families as I walked up the stairs. The nice woman showed us where Dad would be staying with the other men and the private room that Bobbie, Michelle, and I would share with Mom. She told us when breakfast and dinner would be served and that we were on our own for lunch. Until I was about sixteen years old, I thought this shelter was a bed-and-breakfast. Mom told me it was the nicest one we ever stayed in.

Changing locations more often than I've come to understand is customary for a family of five means that I've gone to sleep in a lot of new places. Some shelters we lived in were more institutional feeling than the others — sterile, yet dingy, with white walls. One I clearly recall was kind of like a hostel. Our room was one big open room with tons of bunk beds. We were there long enough to make friends, which, admittedly, never took me long. It was there that I got my first black eye because Bobbie was trying to show me how to do a flip, and instead of landing on my feet, I landed face-first on a fire truck. Dad told me he thought it made me look tough, so I didn't complain.

Every shelter has a time limit. Shelters are there to help people as a temporary stop-gap, provide a little bit of food, and get you on your way. Neither one of my parents liked taking handouts, and both of them worked hard and took immense pride in their work. Mom was a waitress, and Dad installed carpet and did physical labor all his life.

At our first stop in California, Dad couldn't find enough work, and although Mom donated plasma and blood for money, they couldn't quite get on their feet. So, when our time was up at the shelter, we went to live in a campground called Standish-Hickey Park in the mountains of Northern California.

Living in campgrounds was bliss. Campgrounds were our playgrounds. We'd explore and play all day, then build fires and gaze at the stars at night. It was another place of stunning beauty with a stream running through the back side of the park, and we weren't the only ones living there. Some lived in old buses, and others in tents. A primitive campground, there were picnic tables and a few port-a-potties but no other infrastructure. We didn't have tents, so Dad rolled out a piece of carpet padding, and that's where Michelle, Bobbie, and I slept while Mom and Dad slept in the car.

During the day, we would go to the stream to play and swim. As a nudist, Dad preferred to skinny dip, and I wanted to be just like him, so he and I walked around and swam without clothes on. Michelle, Bobbie, and Mom were uncomfortable with that, but I didn't understand why. The three of them all wore bathing suits. I only remember us going to nude beaches a couple of times, and we even went to a nudist camp once, but since Dad and I were the only ones who were cool with it, everyone else just awkwardly went along for the ride.

As we slept on the ground one night in our camp, Bobbie woke me up to show me a large fire across the park from us. We could tell that it was too big to be a campfire, so we reluctantly went to the car to warn Mom and Dad. As we had suspected, they yelled at us to go back to sleep and leave them alone. Bobbie went to check it out while I stayed close to Michelle. When he returned, he said we needed to wake Mom and Dad up again because the fire was spreading quickly, and grown men were talking about packing up and getting out. By the time our parents emerged from the car, the fire had taken over a large portion of the entrance. Several families had already left, but a school bus someone was living in had stalled in the middle of the only exit to the park. I began to panic, but Dad assured us that we could walk to the other side of the creek and into the woods if we needed to. There were crawdads, fish, and other wild animals we could survive on if we weren't saved quickly. If I had been older, that would have freaked me out even more, but when Dad said something, I believed him, and I was up for any adventure he presented to us. Hours went by as the fire blazed. We could see that the fire trucks couldn't get into the park because of the bus, but eventually, it was moved, and the fire was put out.

The next morning, we could see the damage that was done and just how lucky we were that the fire department arrived when they did and that it had not been a dry year.

After leaving the park, we moved to Colorado for a couple of months and lived in low-income apartments. Dad was still having trouble finding work there, so we drove to Scottsdale, Arizona, where I met Byron's mom, stepdad, and the rest of his family for the first time. Dad never spoke of his family much before I met them, so I knew nothing about them.

Grandma Antry was a business owner, and her husband was well-off. I'm not sure what he did for a living, but he was from a good family who owned land near Tulsa. They had a pool in their yard and lived in a nice neighborhood, so when we pulled up, I thought they were very wealthy.

Thrilled that a grandma of ours had a real pool in her backyard, I said to Bobbie, "She must be rich!" Dad talked with her while we swam for a few hours. I didn't like swimming in my shirt and shorts at first, but I got used to it. I guess Dad had thrown away our bathing suits because we left them out on the picnic table. He was always pissed when we didn't take care of our things, so he'd just throw away our toys or clothes, refusing to pick up after us.

After a while, we went inside to have lunch. In her kitchen was a table with booth seating, just like at restaurants. I climbed in and felt super fancy, but then she put a plate in front of me that had little round green things on it next to the sandwich. I didn't know this grandma — I had never spoken to her and never seen her until this day...and I also didn't know what in the world she was trying to make us eat. Bobbie and Michelle immediately slouched into the seat of the booth and whispered to Mom, "Do we have to eat the green things?" Grandma Antry got a big smile on her face and said, "You've never had Brussels sprouts? They're delicious. I thought you'd like them because they're Byron's favorite vegetable!" As Bobbie and Michelle poked around at them, I decided that my new grandma's proclamation must have meant that they tasted better than they looked, so I tried to poke my fork into one, but it just rolled around on the plate like I was chasing it away. We all laughed. Grandma Antry said, "They're like baby cabbages. Go ahead and pick them up with your fingers and peel them to eat the leaves." I didn't realize that fancy people ate with their fingers, but since I had permission, and they were Dad's favorite food, I gave them a try. I thought they were so delicious that I asked for more, but Bobbie and Michelle stuck with their sandwiches. We also tried Grandma's sparkling mineral water. It looked super fancy and yummy but left a dry and bitter taste in our mouths, so we decided that maybe only old people liked it.

After getting cleaned up, we drove over to Dad's sister's house. She didn't have a pool in her yard, but she had a big two-story house with fancy furniture and two boys who were the same age as Bobbie and me. They had tons of toys. We all became fast friends, and I was entertained to no end by all the fun stuff they had. Bobbie especially loved the Big Wheels. He borrowed a pair of sunglasses, sported a sweet tank top, and rolled down the street like a rock star in the bright Arizona sun.

A month after we arrived, we were moved into a house — a golden-yellow house with a nice, clean kitchen, a huge living room, and my favorite room of all...the sunroom. "How fun! We have a room just for the sun," I said. This room opened up to a spacious yard with a tall wooden fence. I'd always wondered what the inside of houses like this looked like.

I didn't know it at the time, but our new grandma bought that house for us. She and her husband owned a successful dried fruit shop that they called The Date Shop. We had a lot of fun with the name Date Shop...it was a funny idea that Grandma was selling dates. She brought us some of her products from time to time, and we all liked them. The dates were okay, but we really liked the dried pineapple and apricots. The fruit came in little white waxed paper boxes that were open on the top and wrapped in plastic. I liked how the slices were exactly the same and neatly stacked in two perfect rows.

Grandma Antry was so excited to have new grandchildren that she also bought our family a new car. It was a baby blue station wagon. Ah man, was it super cool! We could lay down or play in the back while Mom and Dad were driving. We went everywhere in that station wagon. Our favorite place was the greyhound racetrack. Dad would get the booklet that described the history of each dog. I would pretend to read it, and then

Bobbie and I would pick our winners — based on the names, of course. Dad would bet a dollar on our dogs and then select his own. I remember the excitement of walking up to the window, giving the man our money, and receiving a ticket. Dad said if we won, it could mean big money. I thought we were already rich since we had a house, a car, and lots of toys. I couldn't imagine what we would do with even more money.

The dogs were incredibly impressive. I could see their lean, slender bodies walk up to each cage. I felt sorry for them at first as they waited in their small metal pens, but then we heard a whistle, and Dad jumped to his feet and walked to the rail. Bobbie and I jumped up too. Suddenly, the doors of the dog pens opened, and they all took off running as fast as they could. Dad pointed to the little pretend rabbit and told us they were chasing the rabbit. I told Dad that I was amazed that the rabbit could run so quickly on the rail. He laughed and told me the rabbit was not real and that the dogs could never really catch it...then he pointed out which dogs we had bet on. We all yelled and cheered for our dogs to win the race.

We spent hours at the racetrack and went back many times. Though it was always exciting when we got there, Dad rarely won, so Bobbie stopped going. It would get boring and cold, and Dad was usually angry by the time we left. Dad and Grandma fought about the racetrack a lot. I didn't understand why she didn't want him going, except that it usually made him mad. I remember him and Mom also fighting more when he didn't win.

Scottsdale, Arizona, is very hot and dry, but Michelle, Bobbie, and I still played outside all the time. We had a nice big yard that Grandma helped us to keep up, and our playroom was always full of toys. In fact, Christmas that year was absolutely incredible. It was like something you'd see in a movie. Grandma Antry's house had a tree that reached all the way to the ceiling and was completely surrounded by a pile of toys that extended from wall to wall. At first, I thought all the toys were for us, but then I realized some were for our cousins. That was still fine with me because I had never experienced anything like this before. It seemed like we were all opening presents for hours, but there were definitely some favorites. Michelle, Bobbie, and I all received custom Cabbage Patch Kids that looked like each of us, and we each got bikes. Brand new bikes!

Then one day, out of the blue, we left our golden-yellow house with the big backyard. We left all the stuff. We left the bikes. We took the station wagon.

At the time, it didn't feel like a big loss to me. I was on another adventure. I thought, *Here we go!* The *National Lampoon's Vacation* movies had just come out, and we all had seen them, so Dad said, "We're going to Walley World." We had this big joke all along the way of stopping at a gas station and asking if anybody knew where Walley World was or how to get there. It was fun and funny to us. There wasn't any fear on my side. Michelle's experience was totally different since she was so much older, though she's never expressed frustration about our frequent moves. Bobbie, Michelle, and I still recall that great Christmas with Grandma Antry and living in Arizona as an epic memory that is complete and untouched. We never say, "And then we left everything...again," because while our lives were far from normal, it was all we knew.

After Arizona, we drove the station wagon back to California to the same place we had left before — Standish-Hickey Park. After a short stay, we moved into another cool campground called Kelly's Campground. There was a pond with a dock in the middle we could play on. Dad had us set up camp, and Mom noticed that our neighbors were smoking pot, so she went over and introduced herself. They became instant friends. Dave and Shirly lived in the Redwood Valley and had two boys about the same ages as Bobbie and me.

The cool, dry weather provided a perfect backdrop for Michelle, Bobbie, and me to play all day, forging a bond that felt unbreakable. We were each other's entertainment, partners in mischief, and confidants. No argument lasted long because stomping off in a huff was so much more boring than being together.

After a few weeks at Kelly's Campground, we moved into a one-bedroom, one-bathroom cabin on the Russian River. Mom and Dad slept on a bed in the dining room, and Bobbie, Michelle, and I slept in one bed in the bedroom, which was a ton of fun. Grandma Antry shipped our bikes to us, so we got to ride around the campground and over to the neighboring trailer park, where there were other kids to play with. It was summertime, and we ran free under the lush, green canopy of trees. We would climb the apple trees and have apple wars, which hurt, and we got into so much trouble. We didn't go in the river much, but it was right there across the road where we could enjoy watching it flow by. Mom had a good friend who lived in the campground, so she was happy, and we grilled hamburgers at least once a week. The smell of grilling burgers is forever etched in my mind as a happy smell that reminds me of camping with my family.

Shining sunlight through the prism of my past, I see things from different perspectives, depending on the angle of the light. Some days, I recall the joyful moments of playing in the wilderness with my siblings, and I get caught up in the emotion and nostalgia. *Oh, how lucky we were to have each other and to spend so much time in nature!* And then the light shifts, and I see the struggle, the uncertainty, and the fear that was also always present like a current of hot lava flowing just beneath the surface. You never knew when the thing that warmed your feet would bubble up to burn you. My perspective shifts depending on the light, but it's all true, all held there in a prism of paradoxes.

Both Mom and Dad were alcoholics, but Byron was the only one with a volatile temper. They'd start the night off drinking beer, Coors to be specific, and then it transitioned to vodka with Squirt. Dad would go from funny to freaking out in the blink of an eye, and Mom would either fight back or get quiet until he calmed down. Mom smoked pot all the time and blew the smoke in our faces because she thought it was funny. She was usually laughing and having fun or just relaxing, reading her books. She also chain-smoked Virginia Slims. She would light a cigarette before getting in the shower so that as soon as she got out of the shower, she wouldn't have to take the time to light the next cigarette. We lived in a haze of cigarette smoke, and there were burn holes in everything we owned, but in spite of some close calls, she never burned anything down.

When it was time for me to start kindergarten, my parents enrolled me at an elementary school in Guerneville, the town closest to our campground. I was excited to start school since Bobbie and Michelle had been going. I was jealous that they could read and I couldn't. On my first day, I wore black shoes with a cute little sailor-style dress that Grandma Rhodes had sewn for me. Starting school was terrifying, especially considering Bobbie and my best friend Alyssa were older than me and were in a different class. This was the first time I did anything without Bobbie by my side, and while I fared alright in school, I always looked forward to being with him again when we got back to the campground.

One night, which also happened to be Valentine's Day, we were getting ready for bed, and Dad was listening to the news on the radio and learned we were expecting a flood. Imagining how awful it would be if water happened to seep up from the rising river, under the crack in the front door, and onto any of our few precious toys, we put everything up on a high shelf. Dad told us to go to bed but be ready to wake up if we needed to. He would keep watch. He grabbed a big handle of vodka and prepared to play cards all night with a neighbor friend. To help him monitor the rising water, Dad put a stick in the mud near the river. I don't know how many hands had been dealt or drinks he'd thrown back when he realized the stick was completely gone, but this is when Dad roused us from sleep and told us to get in the car.

So we literally just jumped in the car and left with nothing. This was a new extreme, even for a family that was used to leaving with only what would fit in the car. Few words were exchanged, and as Dad focused all his concentration on keeping the car on the road, Mom stared straight ahead, dumbfounded. Water was coming up onto the windshield, and it seemed like we were driving through water that was three or four feet high. The rain pounded our car at such a volume that I couldn't tell how much was falling from the sky and how much was rising up from the ground. When we crossed the Russian River to get from our campground into town, Bobbie and I both looked out and said, "Is that a house? What is that floating down the river?" It was, indeed, a house that was being swept away — one of many that would be destroyed in the flood.

Through torrential rains, we drove up into the Sierra Nevada Mountains with a plan to spend the weekend gambling in Reno. But the storm that created the downpour of rain was creating a snow flurry at Donner Pass, and we couldn't go through. Instead, we pulled over and spent the night in the station wagon in the parking lot of a post office and drove into Reno the next day. The only thing in the car was the baby blanket that my grandmother Rhodes had made for me and a Care Bear that my brother got me for my birthday.

In Reno, Mom and Dad went into the casinos while Bobbie, Michelle, and I lay down in the back of the car, hiding. Our parents told us not to get up because we were not supposed to be by ourselves. "If anybody sees you, the police can take you away."

Hunkering down in the car for hours, we discussed whether it would be better if the police found us or not. We realized that if they did, we would likely be separated and could possibly be put into homes that were even more dangerous than ours. That sounded bad, so we decided to sing songs to pass the time.

When we finally went back to the cabins, all ten of them were gone, washed away. Where one of the cabins previously stood, you could see the plumbing poking up from the foundation, and one had a toilet standing in a pile of rubble. In front of the foundation where our cabin used to be was a big muddy pile of things that the Red Cross and other volunteers had put together, thinking that they might belong to us. Mom grabbed a couple of boxes of pictures that were mostly stuck together with mud, and, except for my baby blanket and my Care Bear, everything else was lost. I was shocked, not just by the devastation, but by how much work had already been completed by volunteers to begin cleaning up.

The Press Democrat and ABC News reported on the flood, saying, "It set a record of swelling to 48.8 feet. The night before the river rose to record levels, rain fell for 24 hours straight. Locals still call it the 'Great Valentine's Day Flood of 1986,' but there was no romance there, not when water consumed the community, causing $40 million in damage."

Chapter 3

After the flood, I finished my kindergarten year in Santa Rosa, California, where we moved into a two-bedroom apartment. My siblings and I stayed in the bedrooms, both of which were upstairs, and my parents slept in the living room — Mom on a mattress on the floor and Dad on the sofa.

For as long as I can remember, my parents never slept in the same bed. Mom said it was because Dad snored. And while my parents were never particularly affectionate in front of us, I can attest that their sleeping arrangement didn't curb their sexual intimacy.

Late one night, after I was already supposed to be asleep, I padded downstairs to get a glass of water and saw my parents having sex in the living room. Somehow, at five years old, I knew what they were doing and wasn't scared or confused or even grossed out. I just wanted a drink, and they were an obstacle in my way — a naked, writhing, panting obstacle. Frustrated and thirsty, I considered sneaking around the corner to get my water in the kitchen but knew Dad would yell at me, so I went back to bed.

We lived in that apartment just long enough for me to make some friends in the building and go to a birthday party at a McDonald's playscape, but as soon as the school year was over, we moved again. Michelle had made

really good friends in Guerneville, so she hoped we would go back to the
Russian River, but Dad had other plans.

What can I say about Clearlake Oaks, California? If I'd thought the new
house Grandma Antry bought us was nice and had also loved living in
the wild beauty of parks and campgrounds, then the house in Clearlake
Oaks had it all, and so much more! Thanks to the Red Cross and the flood
relief money we got from FEMA, we moved into a beautiful two-story,
four-bedroom home that was on the side of a mountain and looked out
over the lake.

There was a large deck off of the living room, and two of the upstairs
bedrooms had sliding glass doors. My siblings and I scattered and scurried
to explore all corners of the massive house and saw that there were brand
new mattresses, and the bedrooms had beautiful matching sets of furniture. I asked my mom how we'd gotten so rich, and she told me that the Red
Cross donated the mattresses and that the owner of the home was letting
us use the furniture because they were sympathetic to our experience in
the flood.

Because it was a four-bedroom house, I could have had my own room,
but I asked Michelle if I could share hers. Reluctantly, she agreed and
helped me push our beds together so we would sleep next to each other.
She was in the fifth grade by this point and very much wanted to have
her own room, but instead, she shared with her first-grade sister and her
Barbie dolls. As part of her role as the world's best big sister, Michelle read
Tales of a Fourth Grade Nothing to Bobbie and me using her best Fudge
impersonation, which kept us rolling with laughter. We had her do that
accent for years after.

Then, to entertain ourselves, Bobbie and I had dance contests while listening to Ronnie Milsap, Tina Turner, Madonna, and Phil Collins on our dual-cassette boombox.

Mom and Dad still had the station wagon and then bought a green 1972 Ford pickup truck, making us a two-car family. And instead of looking for a job, Dad started a carpet business of his own called The Carpet Weaver because his last name was Weaver. His business grew quickly, and within a relatively short amount of time, we were living the high life. Since his business was thriving, Dad was in a good mood more often. He still got wasted all the time, but without having anxiety over how he was going to pay the bills, he was usually a happy drunk. Mom didn't work for a while, so she was able to go on some class field trips with us like the other moms. She eventually got a job at Bob's Big Boy, which meant we had even more money to use for fun things.

In the past, our recreational activities consisted of whatever game or competition we made up to entertain ourselves. Car games, word games, campground games, acorn wars — things that required few supplies and no money. But living at a lake in the summertime, especially when you have money to spend, means a serious up-level in recreation. Dad bought a boat for skiing and fishing, so we spent endless afternoons tubing behind the boat. He also purchased a stereo that had both a record player and a dual tape deck. Bobbie started taking karate classes and practiced his moves on me, only knocking the wind out of me once while teaching me the final jump kick from *The Karate Kid*.

The Christmas with Grandma Antry had been abundant, to say the least, but the Christmas in Clearlake was the first, and maybe only, time in our childhood that Santa actually brought what we asked for. I got a three-story pink Barbie dollhouse with the actual brand name Barbie and

Ken. Michelle got a phone that was shaped like lips that she could have in our room.

Life in the middle class looked good on us. Bobby, Michelle, and I loved our school and our friends and our home. I planted seeds in the little flower beds in the front of the house in anticipation of becoming a gardener. We bought an answering machine, and over time, we filled the house with furniture and even got matching towels, some of which were decorative. We even took a few day-trip vacations. Once to the Redwood National Park and once to Disneyland. Grandma Antry mailed our Cabbage Patch dolls. (Luckily, we hadn't taken them with us when we left Arizona, so we didn't lose them in the flood.) To complete the whole experience, we got a cat named Tigger, a dog named Sheila, and a bird named Tweety.

Timid and ugly but incredibly sweet, Sheila was just the dog we needed. She was a rescue mutt, and while she belonged to all of us, she and Bobbie bonded the most. Bobbie played with her for hours and wanted to take her with us everywhere. She slept in his room, and he hugged her tighter than he ever hugged anything or anyone. Sheila gave birth to eight adorable puppies while we watched, and we kids were elated to hold so many warm, squirmy little bodies. Even with one in each hand, the three of us couldn't pick them up all at the same time.

As they grew, we learned that caring for eight puppies was too much responsibility for us kids to handle. They ran all over the house, which meant they pooped and peed everywhere. One day, Dad came home and accidentally stepped in a small pile of poop. He flew off the handle and literally kicked the dogs out the door. Later, Bobbie and I noticed that one of the puppies was truly injured. His head hung from his body, and its neck was clearly broken. Bobbie and I cried and tried to nurse him. We asked Mom what we could do, and she said he would be fine. Two days later, he stopped moving. Dad had killed the puppy. Bobbie, Michelle, and I put him in a shoe box, buried him in the yard, and had a small funeral. Sheila kept digging him up and bringing him home, so we kept re-experiencing the trauma. Dad brushed it off and said that the puppy was born with problems and that we needed to give away the rest of the puppies because he was tired of them shitting all over the house.

Even in our new and wonderful life, things were not perfect all the time. Having money and nice things only changes a person as far as money and nice things can change a person. Less stress, more ease, more options and opportunities — all of these are byproducts of life above the poverty line. But one is limited to functioning only as high as their worst coping mechanisms allow. In Byron's case, being a happier drunk and less frequently angry still meant he was drunk and angry far more often than a normal, high-functioning adult. Still, in Clearlake Oaks, our family was the best version of itself, and despite Dad's imperfections, he was at his best there too.

On weekends, we hung out with Dave, Shirly, Jacob, and PJ all the time. They were the family we met at Kelly's campground, and they lived in Redwood Valley, which was not very far from us. We celebrated birthdays with them and went to Lake Port on the Fourth of July. The Fourth of July was one of the few holidays that was always fun. We'd fill up a cooler with beer, snacks, and sandwiches and then grill burgers. In Lakeport, there was a large park next to the lake, so we played all day and watched the spectacular fireworks displays that must have cost a fortune.

Dad competed in several fishing tournaments and would usually go on his own, but sometimes, our whole family would camp for the weekend while he was in the tournament. Mom had to leave one of our camping trips early to work at Bob's Big Boy the next day, so she stayed as long as she could and drove home at night. Michelle, Bobbie, and I went to sleep in our tent, and a few hours later, a police car came to our site. Dad wouldn't tell us what it was about, but we later found out Mom had gotten in a bad car accident and was taken to the hospital.

We learned that as she was driving home, a car drove into her lane, so she swerved to miss it. Her station wagon careened off the road and down a long hill before crashing into a creek. She hit her head on the rearview mirror but was able to get out of the car and walk up the long hill to the road. She tried waving people down, and several cars passed before two young women pulled over and saw that she was covered in blood and needed to go to the hospital. She had no major injuries other than a large gash on her forehead, but the station wagon was totaled. The police later told us that the car was almost impossible to get out of the creek because there were so many trees. They said it was a miracle she didn't hit one of them, but if she had, she would likely not have survived the accident. They were certain that an angel had grabbed the wheel to save her. At the time, I didn't know if I believed in angels or not, but when we passed by the area where Mom went over, I could see what they meant. There was no opening at all between the trees. In my mind, I could see angels guiding the wheel, and I was incredibly grateful for them.

I don't know if his decision was divinely guided, inspired by alcohol, or swayed by a heads or tails coin toss, but seemingly out of nowhere, Dad decided it was time for us to move. Not to a new house or toward a better opportunity. Not away from a life that wasn't working. Just...away. We put all our belongings into storage, including our Cabbage Patch dolls, my majestic three-story Barbie house, Michelle's lip-shaped phone, and our new bikes, and we left. The seeds I planted in the garden would have to sprout in time for another family to enjoy.

As we filled the truck with as much as we could carry with us, not even Sheila made the cut. About a month before we moved, a boy down the street accused Sheila of attacking him. This boy was not harmed. He was angry with Bobbie, so we thought that he was probably making it up. But because we were moving, Dad decided that he would take Sheila to the shelter and have her put down. Bobbie went with him, which was only one of many unjust and heartbreaking moments he'd endure because of Dad.

We rode away under the camper shell on the back of the truck, wedged between our suitcases and Dad's tools. The trip was made slightly more comfortable on a piece of carpet padding. Dad said we'd come one day to get our belongings out of the storage locker. I don't remember what happened to Tweetie, but our cat, Tigger, rode in the back of the truck with us. On the first day, we drove a few hours into the Sierra Nevada Mountains and set up camp. It was pretty there, amongst the tall pine trees, but there wasn't much to do. We were there for a few weeks when Dad told us to pick up camp; we were headed to Carson City. When we packed up, we couldn't find Tigger anywhere. She had gotten used to running around the campground and finding food from other campers. About thirty minutes after packing the truck, Dad made us get in the car and leave Tigger behind. Now Michelle was crushed. We drove silently for the next two hours in the back of the truck. Michelle cried for a bit and then tried to pretend she was sleeping. I pretended to sleep too, and I then pretended that my arm accidentally landed over her so I could hold her in a hug.

Like shape-shifters, who'd been transformed by a flood into a family who lived a big life in a big house on a beautiful lake with pets and karate lessons and a boombox, we instantly reverted to being a family who had nothing to show for ourselves or cling to but each other.

Carson City was in the valley at the foot of the Sierra Nevada Mountains. It's the state capital but is actually quite a small city, mostly old and dirty. We moved into a small two-bedroom apartment and bought furniture from the local thrift store.

Bobbie and I explored the abandoned motels behind our apartment building and convinced ourselves that they were haunted. I often had nightmares about them. Michelle found a friend in the complex who we thought was spoiled because she had all the Barbie things we saw on television commercials and was allowed to go to a Michael Jackson concert. I spent my time watching *Star Search* through other people's apartment windows from the playground and then trying to reenact the dance routines.

I'm sure we went to school there, but I don't remember it. We celebrated Christmas in our little apartment. Santa brought Michelle and me a Barbie car and jeep to share...I knew that a real Santa wouldn't ask us to share, so I made Mom fess up that it was her decision. We also got a Nintendo with the standard Mario Brothers game.

On a Saturday in the spring, we took a trip up the mountain to visit a town named Virginia City. We packed sandwiches and spent the day looking in shops and walking around this tiny mountain town. Yes, my father decided, this would be our next destination.

Chapter 4

"If time travel is possible, where are the tourists from the future?"

—Stephen Hawking

On the side of a mountain in northern Nevada sits a town that's just five miles wide with 650 residents, twelve bars, and more eccentricities than any other place I've been — and that's saying a lot. Virginia City was established in the 1800s during the silver and gold rush of the west, so people came from all over the world to live in what became a bustling city. Back then, VC had more than 15,000 residents, and in its heyday, with all that mining money rolling through, everything there was state of the art, complete with lots of shops and museums and enough bars to serve the thirsty lot.

It's not hard to imagine what Virginia City looked like at its peak because even after a fire in the late 1800s torched the town, all the buildings were rebuilt in the original style of old western storefronts. Burning down was a common fate for towns in those days. People would get drunk, knock over a lantern, and send the whole place up in flames.

Through the years, with the mines plucked clean of their earthly trea-
sures, VC became a place frequented by summer tourists looking to take
a mining tour, visit one of the museums, or attend one of the bazillion
parades that took place in the summer.

Home to some very strange characters, many of the permanent residents
dressed as if they still lived in the old west — men in long duster jackets,
cowboy hats, and boots with spurs and women in old-timey dresses and
hats. For visitors, Virginia City felt like a form of time travel. They'd get
their photos taken with a miner and his donkey or watch mock gunfights
in the Delta parking lot. When the trolly took people on tours around
town, Bobbie and I threw candy at them and giggled when they couldn't
tell where it was coming from. The district attorney would sometimes get
drunk and ride a horse through town with no clothes on. He was also in
every high school play for years and years, also drunk, and when he forgot
his lines, he would sing, "That's amoré!" It could be *The King and I,* and
he would still sing that song to fill in the gaps in his memory.

But as novel as the western frontier "wannabees" and the naked, drunk,
singing district attorney may have been, nothing impressed visitors more
than the international camel races. Apparently, about thirty years prior, a
few newspaper editors joked about hosting camel races, then they turned
it into a real event, and it became a big thing. From that point on, it was
like our rodeo. They would set up fairgrounds, and people would come
from all over the world to watch the camel races, which made it the busiest
tourism weekend of the year.

As offbeat as Virginia City could be, it was also welcoming to newcomers
and a good place for weird families like mine to fit in. The streets were
named using the alphabet, starting with the letter B instead of A. The main
drag is C Street, and then it goes down from there, so as you go down

the mountain, you just go down the alphabet. Even as kids, this made navigation simple.

The first place we lived in VC was a green three-bedroom house on K Street. It was built in the 1940s, and I'm guessing the windows were original because they did little to keep the cold out and were incredibly fragile. I once propped my feet up against the window while I was lying on my tummy, and the pane of glass just fell out of the frame. Nothing broke; it just had nothing left to hold it into place. The house had no insulation and only a single gas furnace in the living room. In the winter, my mom closed off her room and brought her mattress into the living room to sleep on because her room was ice cold. Dad slept on the couch, as usual.

On freezing cold mornings, I'd wake up early and put Bobbie and Michelle's clothes on the heater as well as my own, and as soon as they were warm and toasty, I'd run them over so we could get dressed under our blankets. I was always doing things to take care of my older siblings, to make them more comfortable or make their lives easier in some way. I've always been a natural caretaker, and I looked for ways to reduce conflict where I could and make our lives a little easier. To that end, I also liked to make drinks for my mom and dad because I knew it made them happy. Dad would shake his glass at me, and I'd immediately hop up, run to the kitchen, and pour the drink like he taught me: half vodka, half Squirt. I knew Mom liked hers with a little less vodka.

While I loved to cook and clean, I was certainly no angel. It was about this time, at seven years old, when I started smoking cigarettes. I stole them from my parents, hid them in Nerds boxes, and shared them with my neighbor across the street. It's a wonder that we didn't burn anything down since we smoked in a crawl space under her house and in the many tree houses we had constructed. I imagine we smelled terrible, but since my parents smoked, no one noticed that I smelled like smoke. In fact, my parents smoked so much that our house often looked like a bar. When you walked in, you'd see a cloud of smoke and ashes all over the coffee tables. I thought it was so much fun to put my hands up and run to push the smoke out the front door, but then, of course, I would get in trouble because I was wasting the heat or the AC, and we needed to keep the doors closed.

Our time in Virginia City was fun and beautiful. Everyone in my family made friends easily there, including my parents, which meant that they were at the bar when they weren't working. Bobbie, Michelle, and I kind of raised ourselves when we weren't getting grounded, and this free time afforded us some great adventures. In the summer, we'd wake up and do our chores, making sure to pick up Dad's clothes and socks from the living room, clean the coffee table of last night's ashes and drink spills, do the dishes, and clean the bathrooms. Some days, we were each given two dollars, which we'd either use to go to the public pool or buy candy. Some days, I would run around with my friend Ally or go play with Bobbie in the abandoned mines or go exploring.

Bobbie and I once rode our bikes down Six Mile Canyon, and I don't know why we rode our bikes because it's impossible to ride them back up, but we did, and then we decided to just go off to the side and explore the mountainside. We chased a lizard and tried catching it, which led us to discover a waterfall. Mesmerized by the rushing water pouring from above, we sat there for a little while and then played in the water before heading back. Bobbie and I tried to return to that waterfall but never found it again. I wonder if it was from snowmelt runoff or if it was a magical little fairyland that was put there just for Bobbie and me to enjoy.

Behind our house was a camper trailer — the kind of trailer you put on the back of a truck. It had a bed and a small kitchen with a table, so it was a cool place to hang out. Bobbie and I used to sleep in the camper on warmer nights, which made it easy to sneak out and roam around the town. Knowing our parents were out drinking, we'd look inside the bars to see if they were there and run past when we saw them. We'd often stay out past two o'clock in the morning in this wild west mountain town.

We weren't always causing mischief, though. Bobbie and I also liked doing things that other kids growing up in the '80s did, like playing T-ball in a big field with all the other kids in town. We also played army amongst the sagebrush around our house, crawling around on the ground and hiding before a big attack. Or sometimes, Bobbie egged me on and laughed while I dramatically danced out music videos to Madonna or Cindy Lauper. We didn't own a VCR, but we'd sometimes rent one from the video store along with the two-video maximum allowance.

Mom waited tables, mostly at the Delta Saloon, which kept her busy and making good money during the summers when the parades and mining tours and camel races drew in the crowds, but winters were tough. Winters were hard on both my parents. Most of Dad's work was in Reno or Carson City, which meant Dad had to drive through the snow down a winding mountain road with no shoulder. When the road wasn't impassable, it was death-defying.

With an increase in stress and alcohol consumption, Mom and Dad started fighting a lot...more than usual. Dad always wanted to stay in town drinking and gambling longer than Mom did, so they'd come home yelling at each other in the middle of the night. Dad made more money than Mom a lot of the time — or so it seemed from their arguments, but she controlled the money and paid the bills, so she knew how much could be spent. Dad always wanted twenty more dollars because of a hot table, machine, or something that was about to pay out for him. Some nights, they'd yell for a bit and call each other names before giving up and settling down, and other nights it would get nasty. Dad overturned tables, ripped cords out of the walls, and sometimes knocked Mom around.

After a period where the nights were consistently ending badly, Dad called the house and told us to pack his bags. Bobbie, Michelle, and I eagerly gathered everything that was clearly his, fishing poles and all, and stacked it by the front door. When Dad came home, he couldn't help but laugh when he told us he wasn't moving out but that he'd only be gone for a few weeks. He was going to visit his daughter, Vicki, in Claremore, Oklahoma. We had never met Vicki before and really didn't know anything about her, but we were happy to get a little break.

The time he was gone was peaceful, but it went by quickly. Bobbie and I still ran around town playing with our friends, and when our talks turned to what it would be like if Dad didn't come home, I reminded them that we wouldn't be able to afford rent without him.

Being on her own certainly didn't stop Mom from having a good time. One night, Mom went out somewhere and had her best friend Genée babysit us. Having a babysitter was new for us, but Mom knew she was going to be out all night and wasn't sure what time she'd return. Genée was a riot, but she didn't know much about kids...or cooking. She found a recipe for twice-baked potatoes that looked like it would be fun for us all to make together and was something kids would eat. Enthusiastic about the project, we helped her do the baking and scooping and baking again, but we all forgot the potatoes were baking while watching a movie, and they got so burned that we had to throw the whole baking sheet away. I think we had ramen noodles for dinner that night.

We stayed in Virginia City long enough for me to finish second grade and start third, but shortly after Dad got home from visiting Vicki, he got the itch to move back to Oklahoma. Perhaps he wanted to be closer to his first-born daughter, or maybe he just wanted to move again for no discernable reason at all.

So we packed up the truck, leaving behind the accumulation of relics one collects while living in a place, and traveled forward in time, down the mountain, out of the old west, back onto the flat, warm earth, and headed east.

Chapter 5

Bobbie, Michelle, and I rode in the back of the truck the entire distance between Nevada and Oklahoma. Mom and Dad only stopped when they needed to, so we had to make sure we didn't drink too much. It must have been close to the holidays because we sang Christmas songs, turning a lot of them into rock tunes for fun.

For the first few weeks in Tulsa, we lived with my Aunt Marilyn and her family. From my point of view, they seemed to have the perfect family. She drove an Audi, my uncle Jaime worked full-time somewhere, my cousins had name-brand clothes, and they lived in a two-story house that backed up to the fields between the elementary and middle schools. Their dad bought them donuts on Sunday mornings, and he giggled, laughed, and played with them. When my cousin Crystal let me wear her clothes, I thought I was the queen of style. I could tell she looked up to Michelle, and even though she was younger than me, I looked up to her.

We quickly moved into a three-bedroom house across the field from them. Bobbie and I attended the elementary school down the street, and Michelle went to the middle school. Since it was a short walk, Crystal and I played together all the time — mostly Barbies — and we spent about every other weekend at my grandma Rhodes' house. Thanksgiving and Christmas there were like a dream. There were cousins, aunts, and uncles everywhere, and everyone brought something home-cooked and delicious to share. Grandma had eight kids, so there was a lot of love that filled her small home in Wagoner. One of my favorite uncles, Uncle Dean, was mentally disabled and played Santa every year and loved western movies. We spent hours and hours watching John Wayne movies and then playing cowboys and Indians with pistols strapped to our hips.

We stayed in that house for maybe nine months but moved to another house on the other side of town for the next school year. Just when I started making friends, I also developed a problem. The elementary school was organized like a middle school, where students switch from one classroom to another for different classes, so timing and organization were stressful...and I was stressed. On several different occasions, I was too nervous to ask the teacher to go to the bathroom and ended up peeing my pants. Once I became known as a pants wetter, I no longer had friends. I was also too scared to ask for help in math, so I pretended to have a stomach ache almost every day so I could go to the nurse's office. With my sullied reputation and rising anxiety, I was incredibly relieved when Dad announced we were moving back to Virginia City.

Walking into a room and forgetting why you're there or putting a box of cereal in the fridge instead of the pantry are typical distractions that make you feel silly, disrupt your day, and, for a split second, make you question your sanity. My parents, however, had a capacity for distraction that didn't make them feel silly but instead disrupted our lives, and, in retrospect, was completely insane. More than once, we couldn't even make it to the destination we intended to move to before they got distracted by a different town, and we'd end up living there instead.

This is how our move back to Virginia City, a town we knew and loved, turned into a move to Boulder City, just outside of Las Vegas. Upon arrival, we moved into a rundown hotel, where we lived for several months. Considering the circumstances of having lived in shelters, cabins, campgrounds, and old, worn-out houses, I could usually find something nice to say about a place. But the motel in Boulder City was crappy and depressing.

It seemed that most of the guests of this motel were residents, and there were a few partially torn down or partially constructed buildings on either side of us, making it look like a project someone abandoned because it just wasn't worth fixing. Bobbie and I played in those lots quite a bit, but exposed rusty nails and loose two-by-fours make for a lame playground and one that most parents would forbid their children from exploring. I guess tetanus was not at the top of my parents' list of concerns.

The one lovely memory that stands out from Boulder City is walking along a cinder block wall with Bobbie and discovering a pomegranate tree. Its tart seeds were so bright, exotic, and tasty that the flavor left an imprint in my mind.

Whatever it was about Boulder City that snagged Dad's attention didn't keep him intrigued for long. So, after a few months under the spell of this roadside distraction, we continued the journey back to Virginia City.

The studio apartment above Red's Candies, one of the downtown shops in VC, was fully furnished. There was one double bed, a couch, a recliner, and a four-seat dining room table. Along the back wall was a small kitchen and, behind that, a bathroom. All five of us lived in that one room. Though we'd slept in smaller spaces like tents or our car or on the ground, when we were all lined up in a row atop a square of carpet padding, this studio somehow felt smaller. Perhaps this was because cars and tents and campgrounds are surrounded by infinite space and don't give you the illusion that you're home, but the studio was just enough space to make you want to play house.

I liked piling blankets to build a cozy fort behind the recliner, where I read stacks of books. And if having a private library wasn't luxurious enough, I also made the bathroom my private dance studio. Most of my classmates were taking dance classes, so I would go to the classes every single Thursday to watch them. Mom and Dad couldn't afford to put me into a dance class, but I never stopped going to watch. After class, I closed myself into our bathroom, my makeshift dance studio, wearing my clickiest, fanciest shoes to practice the tap and jazz choreography I'd observed the other girls doing. Eventually, Mrs. Metzker, one of the other parents, felt sorry for me and was so impressed that I already knew all the dances that she paid for me to be in the class.

Her incredible generosity was not lost on me, and I was so grateful for the opportunity to dance with the other girls. I later discovered that this was what many of the adults in this town, the ones considered the "haves," did for the rest of us, the "have-nots." I wish I could say that, at the time, it instilled in me a valiant desire to be one of the "haves" so I could grow up and pay it forward, but if I'm being honest, it didn't even occur to me that having more or outpacing my "have-not" status was even a possibility.

Unfortunately, my dance career was short-lived. While running to dance class, not because I was late but because I was excited to get there, I jumped up on a cement block and broke my ankle. I knew right away that it was a terrible injury, much worse than a sprain. I watched class that night, but because I was unable to put weight on it, I asked a parent to drive me home. When I told my parents my ankle was broken, neither of them believed me or were willing to take me to a doctor. They brushed it off and told me I'd be fine, and I tried really hard to believe them. I wanted it to be fine too, but I couldn't even shift my body in bed without wincing, much less try to walk or even hobble to the bathroom. Still, they refused to take me to a doctor or even wrap or ice it. Four weeks of incredible pain went by before I could put much weight on that foot. Eventually, it healed, but I was not able to resume dance classes. Without a cast or physical therapy, my bones mended in a way that left my ankle tender and weak.

Noticing I had plenty of free time on my hands, a friend of my mom's asked me to help her bus tables. I didn't know she was going to pay me; I just loved to help out. Turns out that talking with the tourists and keeping the place clean was fun and easy for me, and at the end of the first day, the owner told me she was very impressed with me and asked if I was willing to work every weekend for one dollar an hour. I was eight years old, and I had my first job working at Calamity Jane's Bar and Grill.

After a few months of bussing tables, I was taught how to serve food. Our menu consisted of hot dogs, sausages, sliders, pretzels, popcorn...and plenty of beer. I was later taught how to run the register and count back change, which seems to be a lost art in the modern world. During Christmas break, I worked directly with Rosalie, the owner, and she showed me how to do inventory, write checks, and do the basic tasks related to running a business. I was in heaven. Eventually, Rosalie raised my hourly wage to two dollars an hour, but I had to clock out by six o'clock because Calamity Jane's turned into a bar at night.

I wasn't the only kid working at Calamity Jane's. One of the other employees had a son named Justin, who helped out from time to time. A scrappy kid, Justin was also doing odds and ends for other business owners around town. He and I became good friends and spent time hanging out during our off hours. I didn't realize it at the time, but Justin and I had the shared experience of raising ourselves, but unlike me, with parents who bought groceries for us, he had to work all over town so he could buy food for his family.

Since I loved working so much, I also started babysitting and working at the local market. The market was the closest thing we had to a grocery store. It was smaller than an average convenience store, but it had all the essentials, and I clerked there a few days a week on my days off from Calamity Jane's. The babysitting gig was mostly playing for me, but I was in charge, and I got paid. The two little girls down the hall were two and four, so we would color, do math worksheets, and read. After I cooked dinner and got the girls to sleep, I'd clean the house so their parents could return to a relaxing place.

A good work ethic is a quality I'm proud to have inherited from my parents. Even at eight and nine years old, I always gave my best effort, and with one exception, I was always on time. That one exception happened the morning after I'd slept over at my friend Roxanne's house in the Highlands, an area nestled between Reno and Virginia City. My parents never picked me up after sleepovers, and her parents had gone somewhere, and I was scheduled to work a shift at Calamity's that next morning. With no other discernible options, we decided to ride horses through a steep mountain pass into town.

Roxanne had ridden into town with her mom before, so she felt like she knew what she was doing. I was an inexperienced rider, but I was headstrong and damned if I was going to miss my shift. Giddee-up!

Roxanne saddled up two horses, and we rode the grueling three or so hours through the wilderness into town. Rough terrain and steep hills made it difficult for the horses to keep their footing, and I had no idea how to handle a horse. When we miraculously arrived in town alive, Roxanne tied up the horses. My horse looked me in the eye and stepped on my foot to make sure I knew I did not do a good job. It didn't hurt too much, but she made her point.

I got into work an hour and a half late, sweaty and smelling of horse. Fur and saddle coloring stained the inner rim of my pant legs, and the moment Rosalie saw me standing there, fragrant and disheveled, she laughed and sent me home to clean up. She appreciated the great effort I had gone to so I could get to work but assured me I wasn't necessary that day.

Michelle was working at Red's Candies, so when I had time off, Bobbie and I would get free ice cream. Red's was an old-fashioned candy store. They made fresh fudge, peanut brittle, and waffle cones right there in the center of the store and in the window so everyone walking by could see. When Bobbie and I came by, they gave us each free ice cream sundaes in huge waffle cones so that we could walk through town and tell everyone where we got them. I guess when I wasn't working for money, I was working for food.

My mother was typically a good cook, especially considering her culinary constraints. Comfort food was her specialty, like fried chicken with mashed potatoes and gravy and big breakfasts that usually didn't start until eleven o'clock. She could work wonders with just a microwave and a hot plate or a fryer. She even made grilled cheese sandwiches with a clothes iron when it was necessary. However, her occasional failures in the kitchen were of epic proportions — much like Genée's twice-baked potatoes. Cinnamon rolls made from scratch were one of the more elegant dishes my mother attempted, and they looked picture-perfect going into the oven, like something out of a magazine. While they baked, we all went down the hall to visit with a neighbor. A little while later, Mom yelled,

"Oh, shit!" so to see what she was oh shitting about, we ran to the door to spy thick black smoke spooling down the hallway in sheets so thick we couldn't see our hands in front of our faces.

"Stay there!" Mom screamed at us, but, of course, we ignored her command and ran down the hall after her into the smoke. I opened the hallway door to the outside to let the smoke out as Mom ran into our apartment. A moment later, she came out with a blackened pan of coal balls that once were cinnamon rolls. Turns out, she'd gotten so high that day that she'd forgotten about them. Luckily, no harm was done other than to the baking sheets, but it was clear the building did not have working smoke detectors.

Of all the ways my childhood felt unsafe, burning in a fire did not top the list any more than being crushed by a horse while rolling down a mountain or limping around on a broken appendage for a month. It was the people in my life, the ones who were there to protect me, who posed the greatest risk to my well-being. One night when we were sleeping — Mom was on the bed, Bobbie, Michelle, and I were all on the hide-a-bed — Dad came in asking Mom for twenty dollars.

"No, we don't have it. Go to bed, Byron." This was not what Dad wanted to hear.

After about fifteen minutes of arguing back and forth, Dad grabbed a toaster off the top of the refrigerator and threw it at my mom, but because he was on the other side of the room and his aim was influenced by alcohol, it smashed into the light above our bed, shattering glass all over the bed where my siblings and I had been sleeping.

We were scared, but Dad kept at it. He was insistent that it was Mom's fault and went to find her purse to get more money. Mom told us to get out of bed, but there was glass everywhere, and we had bare feet, so we didn't know where to go. They struggled over the purse for a while before Mom picked up the phone and called the police. It felt like the cops took forever to get there, even though it was a tiny town, and Mom and Dad spent the entire time fighting while we waited for them to arrive. We thought Dad was going to jail for sure this time, but the police officer knew him and talked him into sleeping in the truck. Bobbie, Michelle, and I spent the night at Genée's mom's house while Mom and Genée cleaned up the glass. We watched *The Shining*, which should have terrified me at such a young age, but considering what had just happened in real life, I suppose I was desensitized to pretend threats.

Shortly after the big fight, we had a big snow, which blanketed our town in a fresh layer of calm, quiet beauty. Snow does that — it makes everything new again. It also grabs everyone's attention and reminds them what awe feels like. I'm not sure how many inches we got, but when they shoveled the snow off the roof of our apartment building, we had a pristine white pile of fresh snow in the tiny front yard. It was probably six feet tall and eight feet around, so Bobbie and I decided to turn it into a playscape. We made steps up one side and a swirling slide around the other while hollowing out the inside like an igloo. It was impressive enough for other friends to come and play with us, and it lasted for days. It was just the kind of joy that made us think things might turn out alright for us.

Chapter 6

When Dad wasn't being funny and charming or drunk and impossible, he was talking about leaving or dying. Sometimes, he'd leave for a day or two after a big outburst, and then he'd come back with no explanation or apology. I wonder where he went and what he was doing while he was gone. What did he think about in those hours away from us? If he was ever sorry, he never let on. Dad simply didn't have it in him to empathize with anyone, even when his actions hurt them, even when he loved them. He did what he wanted, when he wanted, and the rest didn't concern him.

I've often wondered why Mom never pushed back against him. She never once tried talking sense into him when he thought it was best to move out of a furnished home into a campground. She never argued for us to have a better life. "For the sake of the children" was not a concept that seemed to occur to either one of them. I once asked her, "Mom, how come you never said no to moving? You never said you don't want to go." And she answered me nonchalantly as if I'd asked her why she preferred yellow to pink, "Oh, I was usually just up for the adventure. I wanted to see what was next."

Most of my friend's parents had their shit together, and while I assumed that everyone had their shit more together than we did, I didn't expect it to get better. I thought that was just my life, the hand I'd been dealt. It seemed to me that other people had it easier, that their lives were calmer. That everyone else had money to take vacations and buy cars when they needed them and take their kids to the doctor when they were sick or had broken bones. Other people's parents did things for the sake of the kids.

Not that my siblings and I were ever asked, but when Dad decided to move us from Virginia City to Davis Creek Regional Park one summer, it was so pretty that none of us minded. In fact, some of my favorite memories were living in this campground. Located at the base of the Sierra Nevada Mountains, there were tall pine trees, hiking trails, and a pond full of chirping frogs that we would try to catch at night. We spent hours on end watching the chipmunks and squirrels, and there were woodpeckers that we called punk rocker birds.

On Saturday mornings, the forest rangers took the kids on nature hikes, describing all the native plants and animals, and on Saturday nights, they showed educational videos in the outdoor amphitheater. I'll never forget one about the bald eagle. We hiked and explored day and night, and sometimes Bobbie, Michelle, and I would take the three-mile walk along the highway to Bower's Mansion, where there was a pool and a playground.

Living in the campground didn't feel like struggling. Mom made breakfast on the camp stove, and we grilled at night. I often lay on a fold-out chair with Dad and gazed at the stars. We weren't just making the best of it. We were happy.

The motel we lived in directly after the campground was a different story. When it got too hot to continue camping, we moved into El Patio in Reno, and it was the pits. We shared a single room with two beds. Mom pulled out her electric skillet for some creative cooking like all the other times we had lived in motels. There were a few other families living there, so we made friends. There was a small pool, but because adult supervision was required, we didn't swim much. Our stay there was stifling and short-lived, so we were glad when Dad decided to move back to Virginia City.

Back in Virginia City, we found a two-bedroom house teetering on stilts at the top of the hill. Fully furnished, with purple crushed velvet couches, a piano, antique vanities, and a beautiful white antique stove, it had a creepiness about it that convinced me and Bobbie it was haunted. Michelle and I shared a room that was connected to Bobbie's room through a Z-shaped closet. As usual, Mom put a bed in the dining room, and Dad slept on the couch. There was another room in the back, but it was locked. The owners of the house said it was filled with their belongings and that we were not to go in there. Naturally, Bobbie and I tried picking the lock several times but didn't succeed.

Mom and Dad had several parties at this house, and I loved making everyone's drinks, emptying the ashtrays, listening to the big laughs at the stories being told around the kitchen table, and playing poker at the end of the night. I learned a lot about people by eavesdropping, like one couple who told a story about the gnarly fights they'd get into with each other.

I overheard one story about a couple who had always seemed happy to me but became known for their violent arguments. Apparently, the wife had gone after her husband with a meat cleaver and embedded it into his shoulder. Everyone at the party roared with laughter at the telling of this story, and it was the first time I realized how normal violence was in their world. It made me grateful that my dad only yelled and broke things and went away sometimes. It also taught me that just because other people seem to have it together, you never really know what their lives are like from the outside.

As with everywhere we lived, Bobbie and I loved to explore. We found a fallen tree in our backyard and made a fort out of it. We didn't add anything other than a rope, but it still seemed like a magical tree with a lot of rooms and compartments. A bouncing branch was an elevator, a high branch our lookout. We scoured the hillside and found an abandoned, rusted-out car from the 1920s and bottles from the early 1900s or late 1800s. We found quartz crystals and tossed out vintage beer cans. We kept some, and Bobbie tried to sell the best finds to local merchants.

As I mentioned before, chores were non-negotiable in our house, and if they weren't done right, we knew there would be hell to pay. We often picked up the slack for each other, even if we did it begrudgingly, because it was for the best of everyone. As I was folding laundry one day, Bobbie came into the house telling me that he was certain he had broken his arm playing on the monkey bars. At first, I was mad that he hadn't helped with his chores, but when he persisted, I believed him, so I ran two miles to the bar where I thought I would find my parents. Luckily, they hadn't hopped to a different location with friends. They saw the urgency in my face and noticed that I had run far to tell them about Bobbie's injury, so instead of brushing me off, like they were known to do, they said goodbye to their friends and came home. Hoping that he was just overreacting, they told him that they would take him to the fire station the next day to have it looked at before going to see a doctor in Reno. While they believed he was hurt, they weren't rushing Bobbie to an emergency room or going out of their way any more than was necessary. The next day came, and when the guys at the fire station confirmed that it was likely broken, Mom took Bobbie into town, and he came back with a cast. I could have taken a bow just then and given an acceptance speech while accepting my award for being the best sister on the planet. But as proud as I was of myself for listening to my brother and taking action, I was proud of my parents for doing the right thing, even if it took longer than it should have.

As scary as Dad was, I never took shit from him. If I disagreed, I told him. I'd state my case even as he backed me up, yelling and raging at me with his cold blue eyes until I was toppling backward onto the bed. He'd want so badly to hit me. He would get so close I thought he would do it, then he'd throw a pillow in my face and storm away to make another drink. I spoke up to him because it's in my nature, but also because he taught me to do so. He loved to watch the news, and I loved to do whatever he wanted to do, so I'd watch the news, western shows, detective mysteries, whatever he was watching, and then we'd talk about it. We discussed and argued about politics all the time. He taught me to have my own opinion and how to defend it. This became a problem when I hit puberty and most of my opinions differed from his. It also became a problem when my shirts became uncomfortable, and I wanted to carry a purse. Suddenly, Dad wasn't just fighting with Mom; he was fighting with me as if I were a political statement he disagreed with.

Just before my eleventh birthday, I came into the house and said something or did something wrong. Who can even remember what it was? I knew by the look in his eyes that I was in big trouble, so I ran to my room. I thought I could beat him there and close the door, but I was wrong. He came in quickly, spanked me like he never had before, and slammed the door shut behind him. When I finally stopped crying and opened the door, I found a note. It said that I was grounded until I could learn to respect him, and it came with a hand-drawn calendar for two months. I desperately wanted to plead my case, but I knew it wasn't the time, so I went back into my room and cried some more. When I came out, all I asked for was an exception to the grounding, so I could still have the birthday sleepover I'd been planning. Normally, none of my friends were allowed to stay over at my house, probably on account of the kind of family I came from, but I had four friends whose parents had said yes. After some intense negotiations, Dad agreed to my sleepover.

My friends and I played Nintendo and talked until we couldn't keep our eyes open anymore. The morning after the sleepover, my parents left early, and one of the girls suggested that we go downtown to get an old-timey photo together. They said we wouldn't have to pay for it because a relative was working that day. I knew it was a bad idea, but I went anyway. Since we were getting it for free, we had to wait for an opening instead of waiting in line, so we were gone longer than I'd expected. The photo turned out great, but when I returned home, Dad was waiting for me with two more months of grounding on the calendar.

Two days later, I was in my room, and I heard my brother playing Nintendo. I had been bored to death in my room by myself and thought it would be hilarious to scare him, so I snuck through the Z-shaped closet. When I came upon him, I realized that he would kill me if I scared him and made him die in the game, so I waited for what I thought would be an appropriate moment. Just as I started to wonder if his game would ever end, I felt my body being yanked backward by my left arm. My head snapped, and I realized I was being pulled back through the closet. Dad threw me on the bed by my arm, screaming at me and accusing me of playing with Bobbie while I was grounded. I tried to explain, but there was no use. He finally left, and I cried for hours, holding my sore arm and shoulder, wishing I had bruises and scars to show people, but when most of the damage is emotional, abuse is tricky to prove.

One thing I do know is that my hitting puberty was off-putting for Dad. His baby girl was growing up, and his reign of total control was slipping — which is infuriating for a man who demands total allegiance. I began wanting attention from other males and wore Michelle's shirts so that I could lean over and have the boys see down my shirt. I was fantasizing about being with boys in ways that I would never tell anyone. He knew that, and he wanted nothing to do with it...or me anymore.

I don't know why we moved out of the house on stilts except that there was a nicer house down on L Street. Then again, whether we moved up to something nicer or back into nature never did seem to follow a pattern. The house on L Street was a single-story A-frame red house with two bedrooms, but the attic was partially finished out, so Michelle and I shared the attic as our room. We had your standard attic pulldown stairs but beautiful wood floors once you got up there. The walls were sheetrock with some panels missing, but it expanded the length of the house, so Michelle stayed on one side, and I was on the other. It was a pretty swanky setup for a teenager and a blooming teenager. We even had a futon in the middle for a hang-out space. I hung up New Kids on the Block and *90210* posters on my side, and I had no idea what Michelle did on hers. We blasted Boys II Men when we were happy and "Right Here Waiting" by Richard Marx when we were sad. Michelle and I shared the kind of bond that's common among sisters, but also unique from any other kind of relationship. It's true that Bobbie and I played all the time, but Michelle confided in me. She told me about her boyfriends, she took me out with her friends when she started driving, she even let me go to all her high school dances. She was beautiful and popular, and I looked up to her in every way and hoped I'd grow up to be as pretty as she was. Unfortunately, my teeth were all sorts of messed up, and it was hard to feel beautiful with a jagged smile. Still, good fortune came to me in roundabout ways.

When Dad had surgery on his knee for injuries sustained while installing carpet, he claimed disability and got a big check. I don't know how much he received, but it was enough to purchase an '85 white Mustang convertible and get me outfitted with braces. It was the first time my parents ever made that big of a financial investment in me, and I was thrilled to get my teeth straightened.

The new car and braces were temporary reprieves from Mom and Dad's usual debauchery. At this point, their drinking intensified. They were having a lot of fun, but it was showing. One night, Mom got a black eye from falling into the bathtub, and another night she fell into the wall and busted the sheetrock. When Michelle's high school buddies, who were volunteer firemen, found Dad lying in a field, they thought he was dead. But it was all laughs when it turned out he was passed out drunk, and they returned him home with sticks in his hair.

The night Dad flew off the handle, threw spaghetti at the wall, and called Michelle a slut, I had had enough. I stormed (as best as one can down attic stairs) into the kitchen and calmly but sternly explained to my parents how they were doing everything wrong. That if they were concerned about Michelle, they should talk to her; that if they cared about what we were doing, they should spend time with us; that if they wanted us to learn and not just feel shame, they should model that for us. To my surprise, they quietly listened. They even cried. As I walked toward the stairs, Bobbie stopped me and gave me a hug and thanked me. He told me that Dad had been beating him and that he tried to tell a friend, but Dad beat him even harder for it. I guess it's one thing to be upset when your little girl grows up, but it's another thing when your boy in the house starts growing into a man. Dad was like a baboon, vying for dominance.

The next day, Dad left, but this time he wasn't just escaping for a few days. He went to rehab and was there for a month. I hadn't planned on doing an intervention with Dad, but I knew that only talking to Mom would go nowhere. He needed to hear what I was thinking. He needed to understand how his drinking and violence were hurting our family. While I didn't feel vindicated for standing up to him, I did finally feel heard, and that was something.

Leveraging the freedom I enjoyed in my father's absence, I focused on doing things that made me happy. I started taking theater classes, and though I was pretty nervous, I loved it. We competed in a thing called Odyssey of the Mind in Carson City and performed the plays *Alice in Wonderland* and a Chinese adaptation of *Cinderella*.

I was finally able to stay the night at a friend's house multiple nights in a row, which I normally wouldn't get to do because Dad had a one-night rule, and we had to be home by noon. It was spring break, and there was still a lot of snow on the ground. I went sledding with my friend Alexa and her older brother, Jacob.

The steep hill we chose crossed over a street, and it sent us flying over a mound of snow piled high by snow plows, and we finally ran out of steam in an open field.

First, I sledded down by myself, feeling so light and free. Jacob met me and reached for my hand, the surprise of which made my heart flutter. I thought he was probably just excited to be sledding, but then he had the idea that we would sled together. I sat in the front, and he wrapped his arms and legs around me. The sled went downhill faster with the two of us together, so I assumed that's why he did it. We sledded for hours, taking turns and swapping partners until our fingers were numb and our cold, pink cheeks hurt from laughing.

When we got back to Alexa and Jacob's house, we cleaned up and ate dinner, and as Alexa and I headed to her room, Jacob invited us into his. He said he wanted to hang out with us and play games. His room was the coolest of cool. Every inch of the walls and ceiling was covered in posters. His lights were warm and dim. He said he wanted to play truth or dare, and he said I had to go first and that I had to pick dare. He told Alexa to leave, and when she did, he dared me to kiss him. I had never kissed anyone before, so I had no clue what to do, and I knew that he did. He was seventeen, and I was twelve. I shook my head slightly, and he leaned in and kissed me sweetly and gently and then smiled at me. He told me that I was next and that I had to do the same dare, so I did. We brought Alexa back in and played for a while then he asked her to leave again. He told me I had five minutes with him, and I could do or ask for anything I wanted. Again, I had no idea, so I just kissed him the way that he had kissed me. When we brought Alexa back in, she said she didn't want to play anymore, so I got on the floor with her, and we all talked for a while. He said he wanted us to sleep in his room, so we made pallets on the floor. Alexa went to sleep, but I didn't. I couldn't believe I had just French-kissed a super-hot high school guy. Then, he tapped me on the shoulder and asked me to get in bed with him. I got under the covers with him, and after kissing and rubbing together for a bit, he pulled off our pants, and he entered me slowly and gently, just like I wanted him to, just like I had fantasized about.

When it was over, I snuck down onto the pallet on the floor and tried to sleep. Shocked at what had happened, I was scared that my dad would find out, and I was surprised that I could still feel him. There was a little bit of pain but not much. When I awoke, there was an Easter basket on the floor next to my head. I had completely forgotten it was Easter, and their sweet mom had bought us all Easter baskets.

That next day was basically the same. Playing in the snow all day, truth or dare at night, followed by a tap on the shoulder. This time I knew exactly what was going to happen, and I welcomed it again. When I finally went home, I was certain my mom would see something different in me, the way I walked, the blush in my cheeks, something, but she didn't.

Shortly after, Dad returned home, and I wondered if he would notice something different about me, but he didn't. All he wanted to talk about was how all the people running the rehab clinic were idiots. In his attempt to stay "clean," he decided to stick with only drinking beer, but within weeks, he was back to drinking liquor. Nothing had changed about my dad, and nothing had changed about me except the way I felt. Months went by without me seeing or talking to Jacob. Part of me didn't want anyone to know what had happened, and part of me wanted to be with him all the time, even if it was a secret. Having been with him suddenly gave me confidence in my body, and I felt a sense of feminine power. When I was at Alexa's house and she would say, "Oh, we can't do that; my brother will get mad at me," I'd say, "Tell him I did it." I instinctively knew he would feel differently about me.

I eventually stayed the night at Alexa's house again. I'd seen Jacob around at different events, and I thought he would at least say hi to me at the high school basketball games or wave at me in passing, and he did a little, but it was clear that he wanted his friends to think I was just another one of his sister's friends. When he and I finally got some alone time, he asked me to come into his room, sat me down on his lap, and told me he'd missed me. And I said, "Well, you don't even talk to me. Why don't you talk to me?" He said, "I didn't think you wanted me to." I told him I felt like he wanted me to pretend like it didn't happen. And he said all sorts of niceties and gave me a kiss.

I told a few of my friends because I thought it was cool being the first girl in my group to grow up and become a woman. The reaction they gave me, however, was not one of praise but of disapproval. Rather than getting excited and asking me what it was like to have sex, they stopped being friends with me. I hadn't felt any shame about what I'd done, so instead of downplaying the incident, I got new friends who smoked cigarettes, drank, and talked about doing things with boys.

And at the same time I acquired friends from the wrong side of the tracks, some of whom had families more dysfunctional than mine, I was offered a thread-thin tether to a better life. Rosalie and Homer, the owners of Calamity Jane's, knew that I was basically raising myself, and they tried their best to help me in the ways that they could. Rosalie started taking me to Costco in Reno to get supplies for the bar and sometimes took me out to dinner there or invited me over to their house for dinner. We talked about everything like business and school. She told me about her grown son and her family. She asked me about mine.

Their home was very quiet, almost boring. I watched cop shows with her husband, Homer, while eating dinner from a TV tray. Perhaps the most generous gift Rosalie and Homer gave me was my first real vacation — one where I didn't have to pack all my belongings or change schools. They took me with them on a family vacation to Santa Clara, California. We were there for an entire week, and they paid for everything. We went to the beach, and I played in the ocean with their niece. It was calm and comfortable and easy. Rosalie showed me a side of life I could dream about, a life that I could work toward. In a life of madness, the trip was just a flash, a glimpse, a fleeting feeling I wanted to replicate again one day if I could.

Chapter 7

By the time we moved down the street into a white house on L Street, right next door to Alexa and Jacob, Jacob had already moved to Oregon with his dad.

I kept working at Calamity Jane's but not at the market or babysitting anymore. I was making a decent amount of money from Calamity's and buying my own school clothes. I even bought myself a pair of Guess jeans. From time to time, I would clean houses for my mom's friends, but I filled my time with friends too. Volleyball had become my new favorite sport, and I was getting really good at it, arriving to practice early and staying late to practice my serves.

One of my teachers, Mrs. Bush, had journal prompts every morning, and one day her prompt was: When I get happy, I (fill in the blank), or when I get angry, I (fill in the blank). I wrote about how volleyball really helps me relieve my anger because it's a lot of physical exertion and a lot of running, but also, just hitting the ball in this repetitive motion helps to relieve the stress of my home life. Mrs. Bush was concerned about that entry, along with some others I'd written, and she told our school guidance counselor that there was a theme to my writing that pointed to trouble at home. Concerned, the counselor pulled Bobbie out of class and asked him if everything was okay at home, and then went to the high school to question my sister.

Because of Michelle's previous experience with my birth father (you remember, the pedophile), she was afraid that maybe something was happening to me that she wasn't aware of, so she went to my mom and told her what had happened with the counselor.

Mom told my dad, and of course, he lost his shit. When I got home, he took me back to the school, completely enraged, and proceeded to light into Mrs. Bush. She had adopted three children, so he called her a tree-hugging nigger-lover bitch and told her to keep her feminist bullshit to herself. I was mortified, sitting in the hallway, scared, embarrassed, and trying my best to hold myself together. There were a few older kids that were still at the school who walked by, and I was devastated and humiliated that my father was so unhinged. I was already not cool and knew this outburst was not going to help. *I certainly don't need this*, I thought, but then I wondered if maybe this incident would help my teacher feel the way that we have felt and it'll make a change because she's experiencing this single moment of fear of this man, and that's what we live with every day. He threatened her multiple times, and this caring woman, who was so full of love, was crying. My last wistful thought was maybe she'd adopt us. Maybe this is the moment I get saved. Instead, I got in the truck with Dad, and we drove home in silence.

Shortly after that, someone from Al-Anon came to the school and made an announcement along the lines of, "If you're experiencing these things at home, you can come by after school to talk about it." I thought, *What the hell? Who do you think is going to be able to come to school at four o'clock and talk about their parents being alcoholics? How is that going to be a safe thing for a child to do? Have you met many alcoholic parents?* I was twelve, and I was like, *You adults need to grow up and figure out how this really works!*

After that, I realized that I either needed to stick with the life I'd been given or figure a way out of it. I had a friend who lived at the bottom of the mountain in another little town, but it fed into VC schools, and she asked me to spend the night. This girl was not the best influence, but she was fun. She and I understood each other better than my previous friends understood me.

Happy to have a sleepover with a new friend, I rode the bus with her down the mountain to her house. As soon as we pulled up, I quickly realized that her life was at a much worse level of bad than mine was. Like an apocalyptic stakeout, there were two ramshackle trailers in disrepair, a few broken-down cars scattered around the yard, some lawn chairs, and not much else in sight. We walked into the trailer she lived in around four o'clock and found a table of drunk men playing poker. She walked up to a man who I thought was her dad, and he put his hand on her hip and onto her butt in a way that I immediately knew was bad.

We went to her small room in this two-bedroom trailer, and we started to smoke cigarettes and talk about boys. I asked if that was her dad I'd just met, and she told me it was her uncle and that I had to be careful with him. She told me about this boyfriend she had in Carson City. He was sixteen and had a car, and we were going to meet up with him and his friends at the movies and run away. While I would have liked a bit more time to prepare for a life on my own, I didn't really want to come back to this trailer, and running away kind of sounded like a good idea. What did I really have to lose?

While plotting how we were going to deal with the boys and run away, my first thought was, *I'm not pretty enough, and if her boyfriend's friends think I'm ugly, I'm just going to get left out of this too.* You know your self-esteem is low when you don't even think you're cute enough to be a runaway teenager. I knew I could get a job and take care of myself, and with my standard for basic accommodations being a sleeping bag and a square of carpet padding, I'm not sure why I put so much stock into what some teenage boys would think of me. I suppose I thought they could get me home to my parents at some point, or maybe it would be fun to just run away for a week and see what that's like. My plan was flimsy.

When my friend's mom dropped us off at the dollar cinema in Carson, we snuck out to meet up with the guys, and I instantly knew that they were trouble. They were drinking, getting high, and smoking, and I thought, *Oh my gosh, I don't want to run away. I don't want to run away with them!* For someone who'd decided to run away just a few hours earlier, I'd already developed some standards for the company I was willing to keep. Leaving home is one thing, but ending up in jail is another.

When it came time to hide from her mom, I freaked. I didn't know what to do. I didn't know her mom at all, and I didn't want to spend the night in her house without her, but I was not willing to hit the road with some fucked up boys I had just met at the dollar theater. So, after hiding for a bit, while I assumed her mom was looking for us, I finally told my friend I didn't want to run away after all. She must have lacked some conviction as well because we went to her mom and back to her trailer to spend the night. All the men that were there earlier were even more trashed, and they partied in the living room while we went to bed. I was scared that one of them would come in and want something that I wasn't willing to give, but luckily, that didn't happen. The next day, I was ready to go home; however, no one was there to bring me back up the mountain. No adult was anywhere in sight, and this time there was no horse to ride either. We were stuck, and I was not going to make my noon curfew.

To pass the time while we wondered what to do, we finished our pack of cigarettes and started smoking leftover cigarette butts from the ashtrays in the living room. I couldn't get home, and they didn't have a phone. We were in the middle of nowhere, at the bottom of the mountain, at least ten miles from the home I now longed for. Even the nearest house was at least a mile away. Just hours before, I'd been thinking about running away. Now I was scared I was going to get into trouble.

Her mom finally came home in the evening but refused to take me home. That wasn't part of the deal, and she didn't have money for gas to go up to VC and back. I wondered what was going through my parents' minds; I'd always come home by noon after a sleepover. My parents didn't know this friend and didn't know where she lived. In my mind, they had no way of finding me.

The next day, my dad pulled up in his green pickup, and I was both relieved and terrified of what was in store for me. He said, "What the fuck were you thinking? Get your shit, and get in the truck!" When I got home, he went to the couch, and Mom gave me an angry look and a big hug. She asked if I was trying to run away. I told her no. I just couldn't figure out how to get home. When I asked how Dad found me, she said that she called all of my friends, but no one knew where I was. She didn't even know the name of the friend I was staying with, so she called the school and asked if they had any information or idea where I might be. One of the teachers, Mrs. English, who had taught Bobbie, Michelle, and me at different times, was one of my current teachers. She said I had recently been hanging around with a certain friend who lived in Dayton. She sometimes drove that bus route and told my mom where I might be and that it was not a safe situation for a young girl. Dad went to her house on a whim and a hope.

After my big hug, Mom cried tears of joy, just happy to know I was safe. And it was then, for the very first time, that she told me about my kidnapping as a child. About how afraid she was back then and how quickly that fear resurfaced when I hadn't come home. How is it possible that no one in my family, not even Michelle, had mentioned this somewhat significant detail of my abduction before now? Had my parents simply abandoned this memory like they were accustomed to doing with houses and jobs and my mother's parachute panties left on the side of the road? Thankfully, I wasn't in trouble, and I was relieved to be with people who loved me. I now knew running away was a risk I didn't want to take.

One might think this experience would have inspired my parents to keep better tabs on me, but they did nothing to change their parenting tactics, and I did nothing to curb my behavior. Mom and Dad still didn't know who I was hanging around with, and I still ran around town smoking and drinking. I snuck out of the house in the middle of the night to drink with friends several times, and I never got caught because Mom and Dad were either passed out or at the bars themselves.

The only time I wasn't trying to look cool or do what grown-ups do was when I hung out with Bobbie. Even at twelve, he was still my favorite playmate. We didn't have to try to impress each other, and it felt good that I could totally be myself with him. I had one foot running toward adulthood as fast as I could while the other was firmly planted next to Bobbie, content with being a kid.

Bobbie wasn't really happy, though. He and Dad never got along. Dad was constantly calling him a piece of shit that would never amount to anything. Sure, Dad tried to take him to his job sites here and there. He taught him how to install carpet and the value of hard work, but he never treated him like his son, so Bobbie decided to go live with his real dad in Oklahoma. He had talked about it a few times before, but I never thought it would really happen. I couldn't imagine a life without him; he was my best friend, but he was also my annoying big brother.

On the night of Bobbie's eighth-grade graduation, he went home after the ceremony, and I went to the graduation party. I was at a friend's house, and everyone was going into high school the next year but me. No parents were around, so we mixed up a big pitcher of vodka and Kool-Aid and walked to the park where the baseball fields were. I thought the drink was gross, but I had some anyway. We laughed and talked for a while, just a common herd of loitering teenagers.

For all the ways that Virginia City was still the wild west, it had a curfew for minors. We all knew we were out well past curfew, so as we were walking back to the house, we ducked behind buildings every time a car passed.

A sudden whir of flashing lights and the pulse of a siren startled us when a police officer spotted us and found our not-so-secret hiding spot. My heart thumped hard as he lined us up on the curb, shining his flashlight into our bleary eyes. I thought surely he would just tell us to go home, but the officer stopped at one guy and cuffed him before putting him in the police car. My friends told me that he had violated his probation and had a warrant out for starting fires. I then realized I didn't know some of these kids as well as I'd thought. I was relieved that this was my first offense, so I'd be one of the kids who got a pass. When the officer returned, he walked down the line again and stopped with his light on my face, and said, "Aren't you Byron's daughter?" My heart dropped again as I nodded, and he told me to get in the car too. I was guilty by association with a dad who'd made a reputation as a town drunk, which is saying a lot in a town with twelve bars and only six hundred residents.

The other kids lived close by, so the officer told them all to go home. He drove me to the police station, put the guy in a cell, and had me sit down on a bench in the station lobby. I sat there for a very long time, and then when an officer called me up to the counter, he offered me two choices. "Do you want us to call your dad, or would you rather stay here tonight?" *That's a really good question*, I thought! Either way, I was going to be in big trouble with my dad, so I decided I might as well go home.

I waited for another thirty to forty-five minutes for my dad to come pick up his twelve-year-old daughter from the police station. He didn't yell at me. He just told me to get in the truck, and we didn't utter a word. I thought he was saving up his rage and that he was going to beat me when we got home. He's going to show me what it really means to get in trouble. But he quietly told me to go to my room.

In Virginia City, on the last day of every school year, they have a huge field day at the park. It's a school-wide event involving all the elementary, junior high, and high school kids who get together to play games, eat food, and get ready for the summer. The next morning, I got up and got dressed for field day, but Dad said I couldn't go. I tried to convince him it was a school day, but he wasn't having it. Then he told me we were moving again. He said, "We're going to Utah, and we're leaving in a few days." Then I was desperate to go to field day. I wanted a chance to say goodbye to all of my good friends like Alli, Kali, Roxanne, Mariah, and Crystal — all the girls I had loved so much but had abandoned for the fast crowd.

When Michelle and Bobbie got home, Dad told them about our plans to move. Michelle was going to be a senior in high school the next year, so she begged to stay in VC to finish school on her own. My parents agreed as long as she could pay her own way. She could work and rent one of the apartments above Red's until she graduated. Finally taking action on his own behalf, Bobbie decided to go live with his dad, and we all started packing.

I was so used to packing and moving and leaving everything behind that in the swirl of preparation that I didn't realize I was losing my two very best friends. I went from being part of a pack to becoming an only child in an instant. It was the first time I had the back of the truck all to myself, but even packed with tools and suitcases, it still seemed to echo my loneliness back to me. Who would I be without Bobbie and Michelle, and what would become of them without me? Knowing what I know now, I should have begged Bobbie to stay.

Chapter 8

Parents who have more than two kids often talk about being outnumbered, as if a man-on-man strategy or parent-on-kid strategy is the key to maintaining control over the chaos. For as long as I could remember, my parents were the ones who were outnumbered. With three of us there to run diversions, cover for one another, or take turns either taking the heat or asking for things, we'd found ways to get away with stuff even if we weren't getting our way. I wouldn't say we had the upper hand or any real control over our situation — which is probably obvious by now — but life with Bobbie and Michelle provided me with a sense of comradery and comfort I couldn't source on my own. With both of them gone, Michelle in Virginia City and Bobbie in Oklahoma, I was outnumbered by my parents in a two-on-one dynamic — a social structure that rarely favors the one who's outnumbered.

When my parents and I hit the road, we drove by Bryce Canyon to see the largest formation of hoodoos on earth. Dad drove the Ford truck, and I rode with Mom in the Mustang. We had the top down most of the way, singing along with a tape of Reba McEntire. It was breathtaking! Miles and miles of red and pink spires formed by centuries of water erosion. With lungs weakened from cigarette smoke, Mom and Dad weren't interested in any strenuous hikes, so we looked, took pictures, and moved on. We stayed a week in Mesa Verde National Park, which was also a place of inexplicable beauty. The park, which is in the Four Corners area, was built around historical sites of ancient Puebloans where their cliff dwellings still remain. It was a phenomenal experience, but there was a lot of hiking and trail walking. Mom and Dad did their best to keep up with me, but I spent much of my time exploring on my own while they sat on benches on the trails. The whole time we explored, I kept thinking, *Bobbie would love this,* and I pictured him there enjoying it with me.

After our week at Mesa Verde, we ended up in a small campground in St. George, Utah. Dad found some work, and Mom and I went exploring. We drove through Zion National Park and picnicked a few times, but Mom wasn't up for hiking. With no one my age to hang out with, I was more bored and lonely than ever. In what I hoped served as an SOS, a smoke signal beckoning for the rescue helicopters to find me and bring me back to my old life in Virginia City, I wrote to Michelle, telling her how much I hated it there and that I thought I was sad enough to kill myself. Mom took me to the post office, and we sent the letter with the return address of Anywhere, USA, because we didn't know where we would be next. Apparently, that's something Mom did all the time. I don't know how we ever got any return mail, but I still felt hurt that Michelle never responded to my letter. In truth, I didn't have any real plans to end my life, but I was in a sad place where I didn't want to keep going. I was lonely and didn't know what to look forward to.

While Virginia City had an average high of around seventy-five degrees in the summer, St. George, Utah, had an average of around ninety-five, sometimes getting into the hundreds. Dad came back to the camp from work, literally vomiting from heatstroke a few times, and there was absolutely no place to cool down. No pool or stream to swim in, no air-conditioned rooms, nothing. So, after a few weeks, we moved into a motel in town.

We had one TV that Mom watched her soap operas on all day, in the one room with two beds, and because I had just recently been picked up from a police station, I was grounded for the summer, and Dad wouldn't let me go anywhere. One day when Dad was gone, I asked Mom if I could go to the gas station to get candy or a snack. She said that was fine as long as I didn't tell Dad. I asked if she would walk with me, and she looked at me like I was crazy. St. George was a sizable city, and although we'd lived in Tulsa before, I'd never ventured out on my own. Now, I had to walk down a four-lane road with stop lights and navigate this new experience by myself. It was the first time it occurred to me that Bobbie and Michelle were gone for good. I was sad in the campground, but it was at that moment I realized that I was an only child and that I had never gone anywhere by myself before. I had walked around Virginia City a lot, but that was home, and I knew where I was going, and I knew who I was going to meet up with. This new life was all on me.

I did eventually get to go to the motel pool, probably because I was annoying my parents. I met another girl who also lived in that motel, and I got ungrounded, even though Dad held it over my head all summer and told me I was the only one of his children to ever get arrested — a phrase he brought up regularly for the rest of his life.

My one friend wasn't slated to go to the same school as me, but she introduced me to some of her friends that were. Christina was one of those friends, and when we started the eighth grade in St. George, we walked the distance between her house and the school together. I had a list of my classes and their room numbers but had no idea what I was doing. This was a huge school for me. We had only five minutes between classes, and it was wall-to-wall kids, none of whom wanted to help me at all. Christina and I had no classes together, and we didn't have the same lunch hour. I absolutely hated standing up in each class to introduce myself. I turned beet red and lost my voice every time, like all the nerdy kids in movies. I was happy to see Christina at the end of each day and didn't understand why no one at this school wanted to be my friend. It had been relatively easy for me to make friends all the other times I had moved.

Grandma Antry came to visit us. She stayed at a hotel down the street and took me shopping for school clothes. I wanted to be super cool so that I could fit in. One of the new girls at the motel, a skater, seemed cool, so she tried to coach me on what to wear. Big stripes, wide-legged pants, nothing that fits tightly. She listened to Nirvana, drew pictures of mushrooms, and smoked pot all the time. I listened to her advice but did not look nearly as cool as she did. In fact, I looked quite ridiculous. Unfortunately, I didn't have a job anymore, and Mom and Dad had no money to buy anything new for me, so I was stuck wearing a persona that didn't fit.

After about four weeks of school in St. George, Dad said we were moving to Mesquite, Nevada. I was super excited because I was failing science and still had yet to make friends with anyone at school other than Christina. We moved into a kitchenette at the Virgin Valley Motel. At first, I was embarrassed about the name, but I was going to attend Virgin Valley Middle School, so all the kids and I were basically in the same boat with that one. The kitchenette had a living room and two bedrooms, making it feel more like an apartment. I decorated my bedroom with posters that I taped to the white cinder block walls, and the school bus picked me up right in front of the motel.

On my first day of school in Mesquite, a teacher pulled me to the front of the classroom and asked me what ward I was in. I looked at him, confused, as all the kids looked at me. He said, "Don't you go to the church?" When I answered, "THE church?" he sent me back to my desk. One of the girls in class leaned over and told me that basically everyone in town attended the Mormon church. At lunch, I noticed the cafeteria was fairly empty, but a small group of kids invited me to sit with them. They told me that the school allows kids to have off-campus lunch so that everyone could attend seminary in the middle of the day. Judging by the handful of stragglers left in the cafeteria, it was pretty clear who was Mormon and who wasn't.

I quickly found friends there because there was a whole subset of non-Mormons who stuck together. Some of them were Catholic, and a few were not religious at all. There were also a few girls who were Mormon and were incredibly sweet to me, but most of the boys were insanely mean. I had never experienced that before. I knew I wasn't pretty or popular, and I had been ignored or dismissed, but no one had ever been deliberately mean to my face. But these boys weren't just mean to me; they were also mean to my friends. I grew to despise these boys, who were the leaders of the football team and the stars of everything.

One day in choir, a boy I thought was cute leaned over to his friend and said to him, "What do you think about butterface? I mean, she has a great body...but her face!" They laughed when they saw the shock and hurt I expressed. When I told my friends, hoping they'd console me, they confided that the boys said equally horrible things to them too, and not to take it personally.

I thought about Bobbie all the time. He had been my protector for so long, always willing to throw a punch or stand up for me. I imagined he was probably happier in Oklahoma, having two brothers instead of two sisters and being with his own dad. Unfortunately, that wasn't the case. Yes, he was with his other family, but it was far from happy. Tulsa is a tough town. I came to find out through monthly pay-phone calls that Bobbie was in a lot of trouble. Not the kind of trouble he got into with us but gangs, drugs, and violence. He was fourteen years old and was hanging out with high school kids who were into the hard stuff. Drugs that kill people, and people who kill people. He told me a story of a night that started with cruising the strip and ended with a friend dying in his arms from a gunshot wound. I wanted him to come home, but he was too embarrassed to ask Dad, and Dad was not happy with him either. Bobbie made me promise not to tell Mom and Dad about what was going on there. He wanted them to think that he was doing fine, so all Dad knew for sure was that Bobbie was failing his classes.

In the meantime, I had to go about my own life. I tried out for the volleyball team and made it. I hadn't practiced in a long time, so I wasn't very good, but I had a great time anyway and made some more friends. Dad came to one game and was very proud of me. That was the only performance or game he ever attended, but I remember how good it felt having him there.

This school district was wealthy compared to anything I'd ever attended. The school was brand new, and the auditorium where I took theater classes was state of the art. It seemed to me like the kind of auditorium you'd find on a college campus. I tried out for the musical, and even though my singing was awful, I got a part as a dancer. This was a huge production with real choreographed dancing — like flips and spins and all sorts of fun things. I was starting to love my time there, but Dad was not. He was developing a strong case of gout and needed medical attention, so we hit the road for California, a state where he could get adequate medical care for free.

When people think of California, they typically think of palm trees and people rollerblading down Santa Monica Boulevard. That's not exactly the experience I had.

At first, we stayed with Dave and Shirly — the family we'd met at the campground years before. Mom had kept in touch with Shirly through letters, and they were happy to host us for a few days. We stayed for about a week at their home in Redwood Valley, but I needed to get back into school, so we went to Ukiah.

Dad didn't have work yet, and he was in a lot of pain, so we went to a local shelter. I don't know why we decided to go at night, but I remember distinctly it was raining and it was dark, and Dad had his carpet-layer jeans on. Anybody who has laid carpet knows what carpet-layer jeans look like. They're acid-washed with the knees blown out, and one back pocket is half torn off from the knife thing that goes in your pocket. As he walked from the car to the building, I thought he looked like he really belonged there. As he spoke to the people at the shelter to secure our space, this was the first time I was fully aware that we were moving into a shelter and that I was starting a new school from a shelter. In our room, there was a small kitchen to the left and a few dingy bedrooms in the back with torn-up old linoleum floors throughout. They served dinner and breakfast. You had to get it within a ninety-minute window, or you didn't eat. It was food. It wasn't good. It wasn't terrible. It was free.

Within minutes of starting school in Ukiah, I knew I was in trouble. People weren't just ignoring me; the girls were staring me down in the hallway, and it was clear they wanted to kick this new girl's ass. When I got off the bus, I immediately went to my room, closed the door, and started doing as many push-ups and sit-ups as I could handle. I was a very skinny white girl, and I needed to toughen up if I was going to survive in this place. No longer attached to the skater persona, I thought I'd try "tough girl" on for size but knew there was a fine line between looking tough enough that people wouldn't fuck with me and not too tough so that I couldn't make any friends. The shelter had a two-week maximum, and I was up to 100 push-ups and 100 sit-ups a day before our time was up.

The people at the shelter helped us find a low-income, two-bedroom apartment, and upon moving in, the first thing I did was clean the walls in my bedroom because they were already stained yellow with cigarette smoke. There were other boys my age who lived there. They looked hardened, but they were nice. I had brought a boombox tape player from VC, and I relied on it heavily and spent a lot of time in my room by myself.

A girl named Nikki quickly became my friend. She was in several of my classes and lived a few blocks away. There was something special about Nikki. She was always calm and happy and loved bringing friends together. I'd often go straight to her house after school and hang out until dinnertime. Nikki had an older sister who was about Michelle's age. She had a one-year-old baby, and their recently divorced mom took care of the baby a lot so that she could work or go out, so we didn't see her much. Nikki had a lot of friends, and those friends quickly became mine. It seemed like we got tight in a very short amount of time.

I don't remember Mom or Dad working during this time, which was unusual for them. The people at the shelter helped them sign up for all the government assistance we could get. We got canned and boxed food from the pantry, food stamps for perishables, welfare for cash, and subsidized rent assistance. I know we had had all of these before, but this was the first time I was acutely aware of it. I'd forgotten how much I'd missed the delicious government cheese that came in a long box and apple juice from a half-gallon can. I'd mostly loved the generic foods I'd grown up on, but I could do without canned potatoes, which were mushy and bland. My parents worked hard when they could, but we did lean on the system from time to time, and I'm glad it was there.

Our apartment complex was across a large field from the grocery store, and my parents would often send me over there by myself. Outside the grocery store one day, there was a group of older teenagers — about six boys and one girl. I was already feeling embarrassed because I had come from our low-income apartments with food stamps in hand when the one girl made eye contact with me. I tried to hide my food stamps, but then I realized I needed to be more afraid than embarrassed. She was all puffed up and walked straight toward me. She got in my face and started yelling at me, saying that I'd been talking crap about her. All the boys started circling around us, and my tough instinct, the one I didn't know I possessed except with my dad, kicked in.

I got back in her face, and I puffed myself up to appear as tall as I could. Pointing my finger just inches from her face, I said I didn't know what the fuck she was talking about, but if she wanted to fight, fine! Chest to chest, we stared into each other's eyes, and I could see that the boys were starting to back up a bit because this was not what they expected.

They looked at me like I had lost my mind. She threatened to call me out if she heard anything else. Without losing eye contact, I told her I'd be ready, but if she heard anything, it wasn't me. "I don't talk shit, and I don't give a shit about you. I don't even know who you are," I shouted.

She backed up with her fake puffed-up chest, still pointing and yelling at me. I walked into the grocery store, and my mind went blank, completely forgetting what I'd come to buy. I stayed in the store for a while, bought some generic bread and mixer, and realized I had to walk back out again. Fear kicked in this time, so I devised a plan that if she came at me, I was gonna hit her with the bag of groceries and run. I was terrified but ready. Fortunately, they ignored me while I walked across the field that now seemed a million miles long. The whole way home, I could feel their eyes on me, and I listened for footsteps coming up behind me.

In just a few months of being an only child, I'd learned to navigate a lot more than walking along four-lane highways on my own. I learned what I was capable of, and what I was made of. Yes, I was still a happy-go-lucky girl — nothing could change that — but without a pack to protect me, I was also becoming fierce and self-reliant. Maybe part of me wished that girl had tried to fight me. Maybe I was just waiting for someone to push me too far so I could let out the tiniest bit of rage pent up inside.

Home safely, I unpacked the groceries, went to my room, and listened to music on full blast. In a rage, I listened to my mixtape of Meatloaf and Breakfast at Tiffany's, reconciling my outer tough girl with my inner show-girl. It was anyone's guess which one of them would eventually prevail.

Chapter 9

Fortunately, my tough girl phase of pretending not to care about anyone or anything was cut short by making some real friends. Unlike St. George, where the popular rich kids reigned, or Mesquite, where kids were separated by who was or was not in THE Mormon Church, Ukiah was a lower-income town where most of us were in the same boat. Without social stratification, making friends became easier, and a group of us glommed together.

Relationships in eighth grade are superficial, so it took no time at all to go through a few boyfriends. Even though I lost my virginity at the same time I had my first kiss, I kept it purely PG with these boys. "Going out" mostly meant sitting next to each other and calling ourselves boyfriend and girlfriend. One boy and I decided we weren't good as a couple, but we still wanted to be friends. He was cute, funny, and sweet, and we got along really well. We decided we'd walk to school together, but the school was so far away that he had to knock on my door at five in the morning to get the walk started. I was scared to tell Dad that a boy was coming to pick me up, but he told me that if he was willing to meet me at five o'clock and walk all the way to school, he must be a good, hard-working kid. It took us a few hours to get to school, and along the way, we would pick up our friends or convince other people at the bus stops to walk with us, even in the rain.

When Thanksgiving came, my parents were fighting a lot. Dad took off to who knows where, so Mom dropped me at Dave and Shirly's house. Their house was beautifully decorated for the holiday, and the dining table was formally set with wine glasses and chargers under the plates. There was a kid's table set up in the living room, but Shirly told me I could join the adults. Another family I had never met was joining us, and I realized I didn't know what to do at a formal table. Shirly and Dave brought serving dishes and placed them on the table to be passed around. I was quiet and nervous and watched as everyone picked up a fork with their left hand and a knife with their right, gently cutting into the roasted bird that was served on each plate. This was not a turkey; it was a tiny bird with the meat still on the bone — probably a Cornish game hen, not that I'd ever seen one before. I carefully mimicked what I saw everyone else doing, but the nerves rose inside me, and I feared I'd shoot my bird across the room if I didn't do it just right. I cut what I could from the bird but decided to focus on the side dishes instead. It was a long, quiet, uncomfortable meal, and while I was incredibly grateful to have this experience, it felt like I was looking in the window at someone else's life. Everyone tried their best to include me, but it was really awkward, and I could tell the other family was wondering why this little girl that they didn't even know was alone on Thanksgiving. After dinner, Shirly asked if I wanted to stay the night, and I said no. I had longed for a home like that, a family like that, a holiday like that, but at that moment, I just felt sad and alone, and I wanted to be with the family I knew.

The next day, Dad came back, and I guess he decided that we should have Thanksgiving together. The soup kitchen was hosting a Thanksgiving meal for the homeless. For some reason, I was to meet Mom and Dad there, so I walked to this place with the friend who walked with me to school. His family had their own troubles, so I felt comfortable telling him all about mine. It was during one of our pow-wows about family and circumstances that he said, "Steph, we're placed into life not knowing what we'll get but that we have to make the choice to do the best with it."

I met my parents in the parking lot, and I walked quietly to the building. As always, we didn't talk about why Dad left or where he went; we just pretended as if nothing had happened. A woman opened the door for me and told me I had really beautiful red hair, and I looked at her in shock. No one had told me that anything about me was pretty, and then I walked in thinking that everyone was suddenly going to notice that I was pretty, as if it was a truth that had only become real just seconds before. It's such a simple thing to compliment someone that it's easy to underestimate how powerfully it can lift somebody up and make their day. Or, if you're me, a girl so thirsty for any confirmation of my worthiness, one simple kindness can become a moment I'd never forget.

Entering the dining hall at the shelter, I realized I was the only kid there. We went through the serving line, and they piled our plates with potatoes and turkey and green bean casserole and all the recognizable things that I wanted the day before. We sat and ate silently, and that was our family Thanksgiving dinner, just the three of us, a day late, in a shelter.

A few weeks later when Christmas came around, money was still tight. We couldn't even afford a tree, so I took a green garland and pinned the shape of a Christmas tree to the wall, along with a few ornaments. Mom and Dad purchased a bus ticket for Michelle to spend a week or so with us, and when I asked if they could send one for Bobbie, too, Dad said he didn't want to pay for him to have a vacation while he was failing out of school.

Mom and I picked Michelle up from a Greyhound bus station in San Francisco. She said it was a long and scary ride and that she was happy to be with us. On Christmas Eve, two large paper bags filled with canned pumpkin, applesauce, a frozen turkey, and other holiday foods were delivered to our house. We examined all the contents and planned our holiday dinner. The rest of Christmas was filled with playing poker, blackjack, and dominoes while listening to country music and drinking lots of vodka and beer. We laughed a lot, I danced a little, and we had a great time. Having Michelle at home restored a sense of balance to my family. Perhaps because I was no longer outnumbered in this two-on-two dynamic.

After Christmas, Mom and I drove Michelle back to the bus station in San Francisco. Saying goodbye to her this time was harder than it was before because I knew how much I would miss her and how much easier the world tipped over without her in it. I'd proven I could do it on my own but wished I didn't have to.

Mom continued to call Michelle and Bobbie about once a month. I always got mad at her when she called without me because I knew it would be a long time before I got to talk to them again. I was beginning to feel at home in Ukiah, though. My circle was expanding beyond Nikki's friends, and I got in good with most of the people in my grade. In spite of coming from abject poverty where life at home was impossibly difficult, most of the kids I knew valued friendship above all else. Knowing how much we relied on each other, we took it upon ourselves to be loyal and reliable friends.

When the six o'clock news broadcast announced that a twelve-year-old girl had been kidnapped out of her bedroom window during a slumber party in a town only an hour away, Dad made me stop walking to school in the mornings and told me not to talk to strangers. At first, I didn't think much of it, but the story made national headlines, with Wynona Ryder offering a $200,000 reward for the girl's safe return. Then, it made its way onto *America's Most Wanted,* and her whereabouts were still unknown. Our tight group of friends realized just how scary the world could be. Many of us had contemplated running away, and some of us probably should have, but when the police finally found Polly Klaas's body off Highway 101, we understood that there were dangers out there we couldn't quite comprehend. That could have happened to any one of us.

When Dad had received the medical attention he needed for his gout, it was time for us to hit the road again, only this time, I had a few days to tell everyone goodbye. Noticing my scholastic history appeared less like a linear progression, and more like a chaotic pinball pinging from place to place, one of my teachers pulled me to the front of the class and asked if my family was on the lam. Having no idea what that meant, I answered that we didn't go to church. He laughed and said, "No, are you running from something? Do you need help?" I gave it some thought because the notion had never occurred to me or any of my other teachers and finally said, "No, I don't think so. My parents just like to move."

Back at the apartment, Mom and I set about scrubbing the place from top to bottom, a practice that had become an automatic part of picking up stakes. Mom repeatedly said, "I will always leave a place better than I found it." I think sometimes people assume that just because you don't have money, you also don't have standards of any kind. While my family's morals did not seem to stem from any sort of religious high ground, being financially poor did not make us morally bankrupt. My dad, for example, held an unwavering flame for honesty. At one point, he told me to be wary and to steer clear of certain people in the apartment complex that he didn't trust because they were thieves. I asked if we were any better than them, and he said, "Hell yes, we are! I rarely ask for a handout unless we need it, but as soon as we're able to, we work, and we pay our own way. And I have never, ever stolen a thing." He told me that he remembered going to the grocery store and throwing a pack of gum into the cart, and it fell to the bottom. When he went to put all of his stuff in the truck, he noticed the pack of gum, and he went back in to pay for it. It was twenty-five cents, but he couldn't leave the parking lot without paying for that pack of gum, and he never would.

Values are a funny thing in that each of us gets to decide what our non-negotiables are. What we stand for and believe in is personal, but while we might say we value one thing, only our actions demonstrate our true priorities. When my parents said we were moving back to Carson City, it seemed what they valued was family. In such close proximity to Virginia City, we'd be able to see Michelle a lot more often. I was excited to spend more time with my sister and rekindle our old friendship. Upon arrival, we stayed in a motel for a few weeks, and the day before I was going to start school, Dad decided this wasn't the place for us. He wanted to go to Denver. Instead of heading straight across Highway 50, he thought it would be nice to see some new countryside, so we took the northern route through Salt Lake City and Wyoming, crashing for the night at a motel in Evanston. Dad woke up early for a cup of coffee, and when he returned, he said, "This is a really nice town. We should stay here."

And so we did. We stayed in that motel room with two queen beds and a bathroom, and just a few days later, I walked through a blizzard in a denim jacket and tennis shoes to get to my new school. The hotel wasn't fancy, but it was warm. Our window overlooked a golf course, and because it was winter, our view was a pristine field of snow. For a few weeks, it was beautiful. Dad would watch golf on TV, or we would listen to country music. He and I played a lot of dominos, and when we heard "I Hope You Dance" by Lee Ann Womack, Dad told me it always reminded him of me because of the way I dance through life.

Being in the motel on the edge of town seemed like it was going to hamper my ability to make friends, but I quickly got close to a girl named Michelle. She seemed so mature and put together, but I soon learned that she had recently experienced a huge tragedy. She discovered her mother's body in the bathroom after the boyfriend took both of their lives. Michelle's younger brother had been there but was locked out of the room where it happened.

Another friend of mine was an A student, loved by all, and when I got close enough to her to know something about her personal life, I learned that her mother was such a dysfunctional alcoholic that my friend was the manager of her home. She made sure her mom went to work, and she cashed the checks and paid all the bills. Everyone I met there was very open and friendly, and just like in Ukiah, where everyone was struggling, you didn't mess around with pretense or judge each other. When the snow melted, I discovered that Evanston was an idyllic paradise. The air was crisp and clean, which made walking around this spread-out town enjoyable. Walking is sort of what my friends and I did all the time. Our school choir was practicing the song "Lean on Me," so my friends and I walked through town belting it out at top volume. There was a park on the edge of town with a stream rolling under a bridge, and you could go watch bison roam the prairie. It seemed so peaceful amongst the actual chaos of our lives. Surprisingly, my friends and I didn't spend much time dwelling on our problems. We instinctively knew that making each other laugh and creating good memories together was a better antidote to pain than talking about it all the time, like how rubbing a sore muscle, even unconsciously, makes it feel better.

Mom was working at Walmart, but Dad was having a hard time getting work. He was drinking a ton and, therefore, was angrier than ever, so my parents fought constantly. In that little bitty motel room, there was nowhere for me to escape it. Michelle was going to be graduating from high school in a few months, and we all wanted to go see her, but we didn't have any money. Mom also wanted to get Bobbie a ticket to come to see us. We hadn't seen him in a year, and she and I missed him so much, but Dad just kept saying he didn't want to reward him with a vacation for failing out of school. This was often the topic of my parent's arguments. In the middle of one of their fights, I just got up and left. I quietly put on my shoes, and I sat in a far-off place in the hotel. I didn't have a plan, but I wondered if they even knew or cared that I had left. Would they be scared if they couldn't find me? Maybe they'd think I'd been kidnapped like that girl from California. I hoped perhaps it would scare some sense into them and they would stop fighting. Eventually, when Mom found me, I told her I was tired of the fighting and that she and I could make it on our own. I would find a job, and we could get into the low-income apartments near Walmart. We'd find a way for Bobbie to stay with us, and he could get a job too. We could make it work.

A day or two later, Dad said he was going to go to Colorado for a while, and finally, there was some peace and quiet. With Mom and I alone, I pictured a life with just the two of us and thought this was a one-to-one ratio I could get used to. Of course, I wanted Bobbie there too, but I knew if Dad came back, Bobbie never would. Time was, as they say, of the essence, so to move this new reality forward, I called the low-income apartments and asked what it took and how long the waiting list was. It was going to be several months. So, I said, "Okay, Mom, you can do this. Get on the list, and let's figure out how to get Bobbie here." My mother and I were finally going to be able to relax. Time to sweep the eggshells out of this house; we wouldn't need them anymore!

The sweetness of "I Hope You Dance" and playing dominoes with my father reflected the deep love I had for my dad, but the daily experience of his rage made breaking free from him more than a little exhilarating. I saw for the first time that a better life was possible, not in the far-off distant future when I'd already grown up and moved out, but right in that very moment. All Mom had to do was want that too.

Chapter 10

Decisions are motivated by one of two things: love or fear. For my mother, who had to choose between living with Bobbie, the son she loved, or Byron, the man she loved and also feared, making a clear decision was difficult. Stuck equally between love and fear, she didn't ask either one of them to come home. For two months, it was just me and my mom. Quiet and lonely, our family had gone from five to two in one long year that was starting to feel like a hundred.

Fast or slow, time still moved forward, and Mom and I spent our time planning for my eighth-grade graduation. A yellow-flowered dress caught my eye in a shop window downtown, and Mom said she would get it for me. I imagined how beautiful I'd feel walking across the stage on graduation day. That next week, everyone in eighth grade from the two middle schools in town piled onto buses to take a tour of the high school. There weren't quite enough seats for everyone, so we all squished together for the short ride. An adorable boy from the other school decided that my lap was the best seat for him. He smiled a wide brace-filled smile and made jokes the whole way, introducing himself as Woody. I laughed and giggled in a way I didn't know I was capable of, but I also felt comfortable talking with him. Woody is the only thing I remember about the tour, as all my attention was on him, and when he invited me to the graduation dance, I was ecstatic.

Yes, I want to spend the rest of my life with you...is what I thought, but I simply said yes.

I had a date with a cute boy. I was graduating middle school and heading for high school, and I could see, for the first time, a life in which I could finally make plans and stick to them. However, my mother's failure to intentionally choose one path over another meant she lived life by default, and by default, I did too.

When Dad came back before my graduation, I had mixed feelings about it.

Part of me was happy he'd be there to see me graduate, but I was too familiar with the cost of his presence. Hadn't Mom and I been okay on our own? Weren't we doing just fine? Mom didn't flinch or blink an eye about taking him back. I wondered if she had always expected him to return. She knew her place in the relationship and seemed to embrace it wholeheartedly. If Mom was the soil, then Dad was the seed that blew here and there, sometimes off on his own, sometimes growing roots briefly before blowing away again. I, for one, was sick of being uprooted and transplanted; I wanted to be the sun, to warmly shine right where I was.

While it was no surprise when Dad told me we were going to leave the day after graduation, I didn't want to go. I'd made good friends, and I wanted to be Woody's girlfriend. Even though I had only attended school in Evanston for three months, I was voted most liked by my classmates. None of this had any influence over Dad's decision to leave. All I could do was make the most of my last moments there.

Mom didn't buy me the graduation dress I wanted, so a friend's mom let me borrow one of hers. It was also yellow and had flowers on it, but it was too big and saggy on my skinny frame. To tame my wild curls that wouldn't cooperate, my friend pulled my hair back into a French braid, but looking in the mirror, I lamented over the fact that the make-shift version of my outfit looked nothing like the vision I'd conjured in my head. After the ceremony, I went to the dance, where Woody was waiting for me. He told me I looked beautiful, and when he said it, I believed him. We danced to every song together, and somewhere between songs, I told him I was going to be moving the next day. His disappointment and surprise were evident, but he continued to dance and laugh with me for the rest of the night until his mom came to pick him up. With one last hug, we said goodbye, and I then said goodbye to all my friends...again.

The morning after my graduation, we drove back to Carson City for Michelle's graduation. We got an apartment because, apparently, my parents didn't know how to visit or go on a vacation. Mom found out one of her friends lived nearby, so we went for a visit. As it turned out, Mom's friend was the mother of Alexa and Jacob. In the time since I had last seen him, I had not had anything remotely close to a sexual experience. The most intimate thing I'd done was French kiss a boy who'd never kissed anyone before, which made it pretty unremarkable. If Woody and I had had more time, we would have kissed and gone to the movies and spent time at each other's houses, probably for months before we considered going to second or third base. If our kissing began awkwardly, we would have practiced until we got it right. We would have been in a real relationship, but with that opportunity behind me, what I wanted now was different. I knew I would never be Jacob's girlfriend and that the only recognition he'd pay me was privately in the dark, but I wanted to feel desired. To be touched and feel validated for something I couldn't quite put my finger on.

When I stayed the night with Alexa again, I slept on the couch and hoped that if I stayed awake long enough, then Jacob would wander in to find me there. He did finally come out of his room, and when he saw me there, we talked for a while about my moves and what we had been up to for the past year, and then he invited me back to his room. I said yes, and we had sex, which was awkward and unremarkable. I had no idea what I was doing, and it seemed like he expected me to be more of a woman by now. I didn't feel ashamed, but it did leave me feeling a bit empty, and I knew I didn't want to do it again any time soon. The next day I left and never saw him again.

A year had gone by since I left Virginia City, and I was about to drive up the mountain to see everyone again. Everyone in town would be at this graduation, and I wanted everyone to think I was pretty, so I put on a slim, black bodysuit and high-waisted jeans — the quintessential cool-girl look in the '90s. Michelle looked beautiful in her cap and gown, and my chest swelled with pride watching her walk across the stage. She had done it, and she'd done the entire last year of it on her own, working and going to school, living by herself. She'd worked hard, and now she was free. No more school or parents or moving from place to place. Her whole life was ahead of her to do with whatever she wanted. I envied her agency and freedom.

At graduation, I said hi to a few people I recognized, but it was clear I wasn't part of their world anymore. Had everyone else really changed that much, or was it me, the girl who'd attended five different schools in the eighth grade? I suppose I could have discovered the answer to that if I'd had more time to reintegrate myself, but just a month after Michelle's graduation, we moved to Oklahoma.

My aunt Marilyn, who'd hosted us the last time we went to Oklahoma, let us stay with her again, but this time it was very different. She and Uncle Jamie had recently gotten divorced, and she was living in a duplex. She seemed to need our visit as much as we needed her home.

The time we spent at Marilyn's was the first time that anything ever felt like a real family vacation. We didn't have anything we needed to do, or anywhere we needed to be. Dad was happily drunk, and Mom was happily high. In fact, almost everyone in the house was high or drunk for two weeks, including me. It's not that we were all partying together. The younger group had our own sources, but everyone was so happy to be together that no one seemed to notice when my cousin and I played Sonic the Hedgehog for hours on end, and binge-watched movies, laughing the whole time. It felt good to relax with my family without any agenda or place we needed to be. Michelle came out to visit, and Bobbie came over, which was the first time I'd seen him in over a year. Having my siblings with me at a time when my parents were happy gave me a sense of calm, a little break from the constant worry about belonging or the stress over always navigating new places. Wherever they were is where I belonged.

Bobbie had changed over the past year; we both had changed, but our connection was still strong. Sure, his hairstyle was different, but it was the look in his eyes that had changed the most. The twinkle of youth was gone. A swagger and a bit of sadness had taken its place. He introduced me to his favorite band, Pearl Jam, which I didn't get into at first, but it grew on me. I showed him my exercise routine, and he showed me a few self-defense moves. Bobbie was always feisty, and because he was short, he often had to do a little extra to prove himself and protect himself.

Mom gave him a big hug and told him he was the best hugger. Dad was reluctant at first but happy to see him. Bobbie was really happy to see all of us. He was not aware of any of the conversations that had gone on, the fighting about him visiting, or the many visits Michelle had had with us that year. He was just happy to spend time with his family.

After Bobby and Michelle left, Dad found a place for the three of us to live that was somewhere between Claremore, Wagner, and Tulsa. Wagner is where my grandma lived, and Claremore is where my dad's daughter, Vicki, lived. Our new home was an older two-bedroom trailer on someone's property outside of town. It wasn't completely falling apart, but Mom and I had to deep clean it before we moved in because the kitchen was awful, with plenty of evidence that roaches lived there before we did. Mom let me paint my room white, so it looked clean, and I painted the trim and the little blue pins that looked like flowers on the ceiling in a pretty sky blue. It wasn't fancy, but it was mine.

I knew I was going to start high school there, and I was scared again, not because I thought I would get jumped on the way to the grocery store, but because I wanted people to like me, and the thought of being an outcast again was too much to bear. I'd become increasingly self-conscious about my appearance, so to give myself the best shot at being attractive, I started a two-part plan to become as pretty as possible. Step one was to exercise all the time. Since Mom and Dad both worked, I was by myself most of the summer, so I'd put on music and dance for a while to pump myself up, and then I'd do sit-ups for as long as I could, followed by push-ups, and squats, lunges, and whatever else I could think of. Step two of my plan was to stop eating. Through sheer will and determination, I wouldn't eat at all...unless I caved and ate a whole bag of chips. If that happened, I'd sneak into Mom's medicine cabinet and take a laxative. I tried to vomit when I ate, but I couldn't get it to come back up, so I convinced Mom that I was having constipation issues, and she kept me stocked with laxatives. Sometimes Mom would make dinner, and I'd try to eat a bite or two to make her think I was fine. If she commented on how little I was eating, I'd tell her I ate all day. She didn't pay attention enough to know what was missing.

Working hard and playing harder, my parents hosted a series of parties at our house. Mom started drinking heavily, but this was beyond what I was used to. She was falling- down drunk and high night after night. She'd stumble through making dinner but would wait until just before she went to bed to eat. That way, she would not reduce her buzz until she was ready to sleep. After several nights in a row of watching my mother drink herself into oblivion, I asked if I could make her a plate of food, but she only said, "Yeah, but don't put it in the clouds." Trying to understand the gibberish she was speaking, I sat on her lap to listen closer, but the more she spoke, the more confused I got. I made her a plate and helped her down to the pallet on the floor where she slept, but she was too drunk to lift her face to eat. Instead, she put her face on the ground next to the plate and shoveled the food into her mouth with her hands. As I watched her struggle, I was certain she'd choke and die in the night.

Mom fell asleep with the plate beside her. I checked on her a few times, then went to my room and wrote her a letter, which I posted with a magnet on the refrigerator.

Dear Mom,

When you get high or drunk like that, it really scares me. You were doing and saying all kinds of crazy things. Please don't do that anymore.

Please come talk to me before you go to work.

Love, Steph

When Mom came into my room the next morning, I described to her how wasted she'd been the night before, but instead of being apologetic, she only seemed intrigued. "Really? What did I do?" I rehashed the story of all the weird things she'd said. I'd hoped my talk with her would be a wake-up call, a moment of truth, a come-to-Jesus, whereby she'd feel mortified by her actions and vow to make a change. I mean, isn't it at least a little embarrassing to get a talking-to from your teenage daughter? But all she did was laugh, pat me on the head, and assure me everything was fine.

I knew my mother loved me very much, and she knew I loved her. There was even something admirable about the way my parents lived fully in the moment and unapologetically, even if that meant they never learned from the past or prepared for the future. No one ever said, "I'm sorry." We just kept going.

The intervention with my mother had a less dramatic effect than when Dad went to rehab, but she stopped getting obliterated and only continued getting to her usual state of being drunk and high. Unlike someone trying to become numb to their demons, Mom genuinely seemed to be chasing a good time. Oklahoma was her home, where she was surrounded by friends and family. It was something to celebrate. Though its expression was unconventional, it's possible Mom was more motivated by love than fear after all.

Chapter 11

No one expects a knock on the door in the middle of the night, so when I heard the rapping sometime after midnight, I knew something was up. I opened the door to find our landlord looking panicked. "I just got a call for your dad. I need to talk to him right now. Is he around?" I roused him from his deep sleep and watched as he spoke with our landlord in whispers. After she left, he sat on the couch in silence.

"What did she say?" I asked.

"Nothing," he said with a blank look on his face, and then slowly leaned sideways until he was curled up into a ball on the couch and quietly cried. I'd never seen my dad like that before and wondered what could have possibly reduced him to tears. "Dad, what's wrong?" I asked. "It's going to be okay. What can I get for you?" I wanted to comfort him, but he sternly told me to go back to bed.

In the morning, my mother told me that Grandma Antry had died by suicide. Apparently, she had attempted many times, once with pills, another time by setting her bed on fire, and this time she had hung herself from the bedpost. I couldn't believe it. While I hadn't spent much time with Grandma Antry, I had no idea she'd been so unhappy. She was rich and had a nice house and a business. What on earth could have made her so miserable that she'd take her life, especially in such a clearly deliberate way? Looking around at our life and our little trailer, I was confused. As hard as our life was, we always found a way to laugh and be happy.

I was flooded with the handful of memories I had that included Grandma Antry, and they were all positive. The house she gave us, the Cabbage Patch dolls and bikes for Christmas, the station wagon, The Date Shop. She had provided me with some of my most prized possessions and a love for Brussels sprouts. But how well had I really known her? I wonder now if she had ever been diagnosed with mental illness. Are the demons that caused her to die by suicide the same ones that taunted her son, my dad, to drink or to run away or to get angry so easily? Unfortunately, the time for learning more about her and seizing the opportunity to pull her from the depths of her sadness was over.

During that summer, Dad became close friends with my aunt Marilyn's ex-husband, Jaime, and they decided that they could get more work back in Mesquite laying carpet together. I didn't know they were friends or that they even liked each other because my dad didn't like any of my mom's family. He never joined us for any of the holiday or weekend get-togethers. In fact, I don't remember him going to Grandma Rhodes' house at all. He hated every person in my mom's family for reasons I was only beginning to understand. Mom told me that my uncle Don had called CPS when we first moved to California and wanted to adopt us, and at the time, the family agreed that would be the best course of action. For that, Dad hadn't forgiven them.

Heading west again, Mom and Dad drove the truck, and Jaime and I rode in his van from Inola, Oklahoma, to Mesquite, Nevada. I didn't know Jaime very well, so the trip was a relatively quiet one. He didn't have bad taste in music but preferred to drive in silence, so I read a book most of the way. As we got closer to Nevada, Jaime asked if there was anyone I was looking forward to seeing again. I mentioned I had several good friends there, but I was really hoping that the boy who called me "butterface" would think I was pretty and ask me out...not so I could date him, but so that I could tell him no.

We moved back into the same small apartment at Virgin Valley Motel, and I got a job cleaning rooms. I had always enjoyed cleaning and putting things in order, so I enjoyed being the motel maid. I really enjoyed learning how to perfectly make a bed and properly fold towels. Both of those became an obsession for me as well as the concept of turning around before you leave a room to make sure everything is properly in its place. I guess I'd inherited my parents' work ethic and pride in doing a job well.

The year Michelle spent on her own alone had been tough on her. She struggled with money, some of which she still owed to several people, and she'd been lonely. Mom and Michelle had always been close, so it made sense when Michelle decided to move back in with us after graduation. She and I shared a room and a bed. She got a job at a local steak house and had to wear a women's casino tux every night. She looked beautiful and happy, and it didn't take long for her to make friends.

My friends welcomed me back quickly, and I made new friends as well. Mr. Football Star/Butterface guy started being super nice to me. He didn't exactly ask me out, but he did show interest, and that was all I needed. I felt like I had just lived every '80s movie and teenage girl's dream.

I was also very excited that volleyball season had just begun. I tried to get on the JV team, but the school had a new coach who wouldn't let me play on the team because I wasn't there for their summer hell week. I tried explaining that we had just moved back, but she was adamant that if I really wanted to play, I would have convinced my parents to be there when it was important. She obviously didn't know my parents. Her consolation was to let me play on the B team. I was fine with that, especially since the coach was my absolute favorite teacher, Mr. Leavitt. He taught Spanish and always had a smile on his face.

After practicing for a while, my coach moved me up to the JV team, and I was thrilled to get promoted, but as some sort of punishment for something that was beyond my control, the JV coach never put me in for a game. I asked my old coach, Mr. Leavitt, if I could go back to the B team, but he said he wasn't actually a coach, and it was not his decision. I decided that the JV coach needed to know more about me and my situation, so I wrote her a letter telling her that I had attended five schools the year before and that we had moved to Oklahoma with the intention of me starting high school there, but my parents decided at the last minute to come back to Mesquite. I was confident that if she understood, she would stop punishing me. After reading the letter, she called me into her office, but instead of having any sympathy for me, she scolded me. She told me going on vacation was not moving and that I needed to take responsibility for my own life and decisions. The next game, instead of taking my usual place on the bench, I was made to be the line judge for my own game. I held myself together and judged fairly, and after the game, I went into the locker room and cried. A few of my teammates consoled me and prayed for me. They didn't understand what was happening either. I stayed on the bench for the rest of the season.

There were a few cute, crushable boys in my school, but most of them had no idea I existed. Fabian was different. Always kind and cracking jokes, I was pleased when he took notice of me. Fabian's mother was from Mexico, and he was living with his dad and their new family in Mesquite. He was the kind of guy that everybody in school knew and liked. We hung out at lunchtime and went to the movies together a few times, and while I really enjoyed dating him, I was also busy cleaning hotel rooms, trying to be cool, and spending time with my girlfriends, which is a lot for a teenage girl to juggle. Fabian and I decided together that we should break up and remain friends, but we still had a crush on each other and talked about whether or not we should get back together. Young love tends to be fickle that way.

We were still in that liminal space between friends and dating when the choice to be anything with Fabian disappeared. I was in English class when Crystal, a girl I'd been really close to the first time that I lived there, came into class. Her face was frozen into a look of astonishment, but the kind where you don't like the news. I'd seen that look before, one of horror and disbelief. Since she was prone to getting high before school, I tried briefly to rationalize that she'd just gotten too high to cope, but she looked right at me and said, "I'm so sorry." I was like, *what did you do? Why are you so sorry?* The teacher asked Crystal to sit down, but instead, she walked directly to me in the middle of the class and said, "I was just up at the nurse's office, and I heard that Fabian killed himself." I felt like I didn't hear her, but at the same time, my whole body went numb. The teacher asked if I needed to go to the bathroom, and I said, "I don't think so." She said, "Stephanie, I think you need to go to the bathroom, and Crystal can go with you."

Crystal and I hadn't talked much since I moved back, so I was confused about why she was hugging me. *What a hypocrite,* I thought to myself. *You didn't like me dating him, and you didn't even like him!* Then I thought, *Okay, it's okay. Everything's going to be okay.* We walked out into the hallway, and I saw people coming out of the classrooms with the same look that Crystal had, and I realized what she said must be true.

How could he be gone? I'd just spoken to him the day before, and he was happy. Unable to process any of it, I left the school and started walking. I walked miles and miles until I got to the motel, but I didn't want to go home, so I turned around and walked halfway across town again to

Crystal's house. Crystal and another friend, Desiré, hugged me, and we talked about how funny Fabian was and how nobody expected him to kill himself. Eventually, my mom came to get me, but she didn't ask me how I'd gotten anywhere or what I had done all afternoon; we just quietly drove home. I don't think she knew Fabian was my boyfriend. She just knew that someone at school had died by suicide.

Fabian's family, who I'd never met, were Catholic and held a traditional Catholic service just for the family, but the graveside service was open to the public. On the day of his graveside service, I went to school, and then the entire school walked down the hill to the graveyard. Some of the boys who were his best friends were the pallbearers. I wondered how they had the strength, not the physical strength because he was a small-ish guy, but the emotional strength not to fall over, weakened by grief.

Crystal wore a long trench coat and had tissues and a compact mirror in her pockets. When she handed me a tissue and the compact mirror and told me my makeup was running, I felt nothing but rage for her. I wanted to say, "Fuck you. You didn't even like him! You shouldn't be here!" But I realized she was mourning because he was somebody she knew too. She was just trying to help me.

Like an unexpected knock at midnight, the news of Fabian's death, where he was in my life one day and then never again, was a strange thing to adjust to. Not only was he there and then gone, but he took a piece of me with him. Our private jokes and conversations that were just between us were now missing. They were hearsay, a memory that could be forgotten in time without the constant rehashing and cajoling that happens between friends. If this was how I felt about losing Fabian, I could only begin to imagine what it felt like for my dad to lose his mother, someone he not only shared a lifetime of memories with but was the connection to his past.

There and gone, there and gone — this was a thought that ran through my mind. And while I was still very much alive and breathing, hadn't I been the one who'd been there and then been gone so many times before? How many times had I moved away and left all my friends behind? Sometimes I left without saying goodbye. It was then I realized that while Fabian was my only friend who'd died, I'd lost every single person I'd been friends with. And in turn, they'd lost me too. They'd also been abandoned; I was there one moment, then gone the next and took small pieces and memories of everyone I'd known with me.

The longer we stayed in Mesquite, I felt like these were my people, and this was my home. Who knows if it was out of pity over my loss of Fabian, but after his death, everyone was nice to me. For once, I belonged somewhere, and having Michelle living with us again gave me a lot of comfort at home. I loved sharing a room with her, and even though we had to share a bed, I'd just curl up in the corner and let her sleep when she took up all the bed. As I grew into my teenage years, the five-year age gap between us shrank. We could talk about who we were dating or who we were interested in dating — the kinds of conversations I would never have had with Bobbie at that age. I was moving toward adulthood, and Michelle was still trying to figure out how to be grown.

"There's a guy I've been seeing named Jake," Michelle confided in me after inviting me to have lunch with her. Going to restaurants was not something we did, so it seemed like a special occasion. I already knew exactly which Jake she was talking about because even though he was a year older than me, I had had a class with him. Jake was really cute but completely lost in life. All he wanted to do was party, so he dropped out of school for the second time. "The thing is,..." Michelle said, "I'm pregnant." Ah, the restaurant lunch was starting to make sense. Reaching for her hand, I told her I'd support her in any way I could, no matter her decision

— to keep it or not. I was afraid for her because I knew Dad would be really mad and that she couldn't afford to raise a kid on her own, and I imagined that Jake would want nothing to do with it. And abortion would make the most sense, so I assumed that's what she'd choose. Even though I wasn't having sex at the time, I thought about how if this happened to me, if I got pregnant from one of the Jakes or Jacobs of the world, in spite of the difficulty, I would keep the baby. I knew how to work and was confident I could take care of myself.

"I know he's been cheating on me," she continued, "and I haven't figured out what I want to do yet." Michelle made me promise not to tell Mom and Dad yet, but she knew that she was going to have to do it soon.

Things at home had been relatively calm for a while. Mom was waiting tables and working in the kitchen at the Virgin River casino. Dad and Jamie had been right about there being enough steady work in Mesquite, and Dad was making enough money not to be pissed off all the time. He still came home yelling for twenty more dollars every now and then, and one of those nights, he actually hit the jackpot for $5,000 and bought a Nissan Stanza — another gamble that paid off. Knowing his peace is circumstantial, I knew things would turn upside down when he found out about the baby.

When Michelle told our parents about her pregnancy, Mom didn't say anything at first. She usually let Dad handle everything. It's possible that Michelle had actually told Mom first because we almost always ran everything past her to gauge when and how to talk to Dad. He was calm at first but adamant that she needed to have an abortion. He knew that Jake the Snake (as he often called him) would never take care of the baby and that Michelle didn't even have the means to take care of herself.

Clearly upset, Michelle said she needed to think about it but that she thought she wanted to keep the baby...and after a few weeks of arguing, that was her final decision.

Dad's reaction to that was pure rage, and he told Michelle that she couldn't live with us — that he didn't want to raise any more babies. He eventually backed off and started to get excited. Mom and Dad liked seeing her belly grow, but Dad regularly threw it in her face that he was going to have to raise her baby.

Meanwhile, Dad had been talking to his sister about his mother's estate. Grandma Antry didn't leave millions behind, but she had enough that Dad started dreaming of new opportunities. Money isn't the answer to everything, but it provides a person with choices they wouldn't have had otherwise. In a more practical vision, Dad considered building a house at the bottom of the mountain just outside of town. I'd still go to high school in Mesquite, but we'd have an Arizona address that would give me free in-state tuition for college. This felt like a great idea to me, so I started looking around and found that Flagstaff was a beautiful college town. Then, his dreaming took him all the way to thoughts of a home in the jungles of Belize, and I tried to envision what living in a jungle would be like, surrounded by monkeys and sidestepping snakes on the path to gather water. Somewhere between practicality and fantasy, Dad settled on a plan that proved to be neither. Once again, we packed what we could fit in the truck, and the four of us, soon to be five, headed to Graham, Texas, to live on Possum Kingdom Lake, which sounded more like a joke than a destination.

Chapter 12

We made a few stops along the way to Texas; the first one was in Scottsdale to visit Lisa, Dad's sister. They'd never gotten along very well, and now they had Grandma Antry's inheritance to fight over. After multiple arguments about jewelry, furniture, and other valuable assets that Grandma explicitly left to Lisa, we were on our way. Dad also had two brothers — one who died in his 20s and another one I had never met and hardly ever heard about, but he was still getting his share of the inheritance.

Our stop in White's City, New Mexico, led to a day of hiking and exploring Carlsbad Caverns before heading to a motel for the night. I had just settled into a bath after a day of sweating in the sun when I heard a knock at the door and men talking. A few minutes later, Mom told me I had to get dressed. The sheriff had come to tell us we either needed to leave town or charges would be pressed against Dad for sexual harassment. Apparently, it's not okay to ask a bartender to show him her tits. This was a common catchphrase for Dad, and in places like Virginia City, most people would just laugh it off or kick him out of the bar, but in Whites City, New Mexico, the bartender happened to be the sheriff's daughter. We packed up the car in the dark and headed out of town.

Two days later, we arrived in Mineral Wells, Texas. In its prime, Mineral Wells had been a thriving western town. It was founded as a military camp but became famous for its mineral springs, and through the early 1900s, it was a hot spot for celebrities like Judy Garland and Will Rogers. In the middle of town stood a huge, opulent art deco hotel called The Baker Hotel that once hosted Marilyn Monroe and JFK. By the time we got there, most of the town was boarded up and falling apart. The old Baker Hotel was a skeletal reminder of what it once was, and I could feel the dread and sorrow as we pulled into town. We got a room at the Radisson, which seemed like a fancy choice until we entered the damp, smelly lobby. Reminiscent of our Wyoming stop, Mineral Wells started to grow on Dad, and he considered staying. In all the moves, I'd never spoken up about being uncomfortable, but Mineral Wells, Texas, was not a place I wanted to call my home. Something about it, that I couldn't put my finger on exactly, felt dangerous to me. The energy there felt dark and heavy, like I'd have to trade in my push-up routine for a handgun.

Thankfully, Dad wanted to be closer to the lake, so we took a drive. After about an hour of following behind Dad, he pulled over and said, "What did you think?" "Uh, of what?" was my answer. "That town back there, the one with the blinking light. That's Graford. That's where you're going to go to school." I needed another look, so we circled back and headed to the gas station restaurant for lunch. The choice of restaurant was not reflective of our culinary ineptitude; we stopped there because it was the only restaurant in town. During lunch, the waitress told us that the school was right down the street. There's that word again...THE school, like THE church. In Graford, the school included all grades K-12 in the same building. "The mascot is the Jackrabbits!" our waitress shared with enthusiasm. I looked at my dad and wondered why Belize and Flagstaff had been taken off the list of possibilities.

After lunch, we drove for another twenty minutes or so and got a hotel room on the lake. It was spring, and it was beautiful, so I was happy.

Mom teamed up with a realtor and quickly found a house she loved that she and my dad could afford to buy. For once, I didn't mind starting school from a hotel room because I knew it was temporary. The house they bought was a tidy three-bedroom, two-bath with a well-loved yard. There were flower beds all around the house and a stone walkway and seating area. In the front yard, there were two full-grown hawthorn trees that bloomed fragrant white flowers every spring. You could even see the lake and walk to the boat dock from our front door.

It wasn't a new house, and it wasn't as big as the lake house we moved into on flood relief funds, but it was ours, and we were proud. Dad let me pick out wallpaper for my bedroom, and we bought all new furniture for every room in the house. This was the first time my parents had ever purchased a single new piece of furniture. Michelle and I both got daybeds, and I picked out a dresser that had a hutch over it and a computer desk with the hopes that we would get a computer one day. The best piece of furniture we bought was an oak armoire to hold the baby's clothes, along with a crib to go into Michelle's room. With her belly getting rounder by the day, Michelle asked me to be her birthing coach. We went to a few classes together, but she couldn't handle the graphic birthing videos and figured we'd gotten the gist of the breathing thing. Having zero idea what to expect during childbirth, I thought we should keep going to the classes, but I figured it was her body, and the doctors and nurses would likely help us through it.

On my first day at the school in Graford, a girl named Lacy, with big red hair, swung a desk around and told me to sit with their group in home ec class. She introduced me to Rachel, and they began talking about the party they had the weekend before. I figured I fit into this group and this school as well or better than I did in Mesquite. Rachel and I quickly discovered she lived right down the street from me.

Everyone in my class was talking about the kids who'd recently gotten suspended for hazing someone in the school gym. I learned this was a long-standing tradition, but someone had gotten hurt, so the school was cracking down on it. One of the girls who was suspended had a role in the school play, so the theater teacher asked if I was interested in taking the role. They were rehearsing for *Henry VIII* and needed me to play Anne Boleyn. I was ecstatic but a little anxious that I had to kiss a guy named Cleve and that the play was to be performed in a regional competition. It helped that Lacy and Rachel were also in the show, and I got to wear a beautiful fifteenth-century-style dress. We performed the play to the school to rave reviews and took our show on the road for the competition. We didn't win, but the bonding experience of staying in a hotel with my new friends was priceless.

Lacy began talking about her birthday party that was coming up. She was going to have a slumber party at her dad's house on the other side of the lake, and both boys and girls were going to be invited. I was nervous to ask Dad, but he said it was fine as long as her parents were going to be there all night.

Wow, I guess I'm in high school now.

The party was fun. We ran around being silly and stayed up all night. I developed a crush on a boy named Lance. He was cute and jovial with a nice smile. His brother Geremiah seemed to like me, but I wasn't into him.

When Monday came around, the whole school was talking about how the new girl slept with Geremiah. Seeing as how this tiny town only had one new girl, I confronted him, and he just smiled and said, "Yeah, I made it up. I mean, wouldn't you want people to think you had sex with a girl like you?" I laughed and was weirdly honored but told him he needed to tell everyone the truth. It didn't take long for the rumors to go away, and Geremiah and I became friends.

One week later, there was a tragic accident. Lance and a few of his buddies were speeding down a dirt road and flipped their car. One of the guys didn't make it. Much like when Fabian died, the whole school was thrust into mourning. I'd never met the boy, but I knew how everyone felt. Everyone except Lance, that is. He was the one driving the car, and I'm not sure I ever saw him smile again.

When Michelle started having heavy contractions, Mom and I drove her into Mineral Wells. Although it was an hour away, it had the closest hospital, and we didn't want to do a roadside delivery. Because Michelle wasn't far enough along in her progress, we had to pass the time until she could be admitted, and we walked in the park, ate some pineapple, and of course, got takeout from Whataburger. We checked in several times to see if she was dilated enough but were sent away to go walk the park some more. When she was finally admitted, the doctor told Michelle that her T-cell count was too low for her to have an epidural, so she was going to have to deliver the baby without it. They gave her an oral pain reliever, and then it was my time to shine. I did everything I could, from rubbing her back to trying to help with her breathing, but I really wished we had continued those classes. Michelle was yelling, saying something about a gun, and I knew it was time for Mom to help. It was far from an easy birth. Michelle was scared, and the baby was big. When the baby started to crown, I was mesmerized, and it was a good thing that Mom was there because I abandoned Michelle's side and watched as this beautiful little human came into our world. Michelle named her baby Hailey Mariah Hoffman, and I wanted to hold her as much as possible. I wanted her to know that I was her aunt and that she was the most loved person on the planet.

After Hailey and Michelle came home, our lives all changed. I was sixteen, and Michelle was twenty, and we had no idea what we were in for when it came to caring for an infant. Dad instantly fell in love with Hailey, and from the moment she came home, Hailey could do no wrong. It's hard to believe that less than a year ago, he'd yelled at Michelle to get an abortion because from the moment he laid eyes on Hailey, he was in love.

I started looking for a job when school let out for summer, but Dad told me that this was my one opportunity not to work. He wanted me to enjoy the summer and be a kid for once. Mom took me to the flower market in Weatherford, and I spent every morning tending flowers and watering my huge garden with fresh lake water. I swam with Rachel in the afternoons, and I actually got a tan on my fair skin that summer! I had to babysit, which was annoying, but I had more free time than ever before, so that wasn't the trouble. It was that I had no idea how to handle a newborn baby. I was terrified she would choke, and if she died, it would be all my fault. Fortunately, I managed to keep Hailey alive.

Mom talked Dad into getting a plane ticket for Bobbie to come visit, and he even drove to Fort Worth to pick him up from the airport. He must have been in a great mood because they came home with a ski boat. Dad took us all out to eat at a restaurant, which wouldn't seem like a big deal, but we never did things like that. In Texas, minors can drink if they have a parent present, so Dad let Bobbie have a beer.

We were all living it up, except for Michelle. She missed the friends she grew up with in Virginia City, and since she was only going back and forth between waitressing and being a mom, she didn't have time to make new friends in Texas, so she moved in with Jake's mom in Carson City.

With Michelle and Hailey gone, Mom, Dad, and I went to Corpus Christi for a short vacation. We rented a condo for the weekend, ate at nice restaurants, went out to the dog track, and spent the weekend on the beach. I'm the only strawberry blonde in my family, so when a family of five redheads walked by, Dad joked, "Hey, there goes your family." This sent us into fits of laughter, and I remember this trip as one of the times I spent with my parents when I actually felt content. Nothing missing, nothing to strive for, just content.

Back at home, Dad spent a lot of time out on the boat. We went with him sometimes, but he really loved to fish and find his peace on the water. Unfortunately, there wasn't much work for him, and I guess the inheritance money had run out, so he pawned the boat. He also pawned his tools, which further narrowed his choices.

Since Dad paid cash for our house, all they had to pay were utility bills, HOA fees, and taxes. He knew a guy in Tulsa whom he could work for and borrow tools from, so before the next school year started, we packed up and moved to Oklahoma. We left everything behind again, but this time, the house was still ours. We simply locked up and drove away.

Chapter 13

Like Virginia City, Wagoner, Oklahoma, was an anchor for me. It's where my grandma lived for thirty years, where I'd spent a handful of holidays, where I'd run around with cousins or walk to Maple Park and play freely with no worries. But when we moved to Wagoner, I had mixed feelings. My cousin Crystal and I joked that there was nothing to do in Wagoner but go to church or hang out at the car wash on Friday nights. It was a far cry from lake life.

Mom found us a two-bedroom trailer near Fort Gibson Lake. Unlike a normal trailer park, where the homes lined up in rows, this place had a narrow road that meandered through the woods, winding around old trailers and a few neglected houses.

My cousin Zac, who I didn't know that well but was just a year younger than me, lived in Wagoner, so we spent a lot of time together. Zac possessed the ability to make me laugh so hard that I couldn't breathe, and once he discovered this superpower, he made it a point to do this as often as he could. Over the summer, Zac and I became very close, and by the time school started, it only made sense for me to sit with him at lunch and hang out with all his friends.

My reliance on Zac was only part of the reason I didn't venture out to make any girlfriends. I was also friendless because, according to Wagoner standards, where conformity was king, I was a weirdo. Before leaving Possum Kingdom, Rachel and I made a pact to buy all our clothes at thrift stores, so I showed up in small-town Wagoner wearing shiny, sage-colored pants or bright green corduroys with hippy shirts and a hairstyle that screamed, "Look at me; I'm cute and different." And also, "What do you think you're looking at?"

I would never have had the guts to show up to a new school like that if I didn't think that Rachel was doing the same thing…we had promised each other. I also knew that no matter what, I had Zac. He was the safety blanket I hadn't experienced since Bobbie lived at home. I probably would have chickened out, looked around to see what I needed to wear to fit in, and done that, but we didn't have any money for new clothes.

A guy named Nathan Deitzel sat behind me in chemistry class and helped me a bit. Nathan was tall and would have been shy if he hadn't been born and raised in Wagoner, but he was also funny and very sweet. We laughed that in Oklahoma, there was no distinction between tin and ten because southerners pronounced the two the same and also added all sorts of extra vowels, which made both words sound like teeyan.

When Nathan invited me to a concert with him and his brothers — a music festival in Tulsa put on by a radio station — I was sure my dad would say no to me riding around with a car full of boys. But, after some convincing and assuring him that Zac thought Nathan was safe, Dad agreed to let me go. It helped that I wasn't going to have to pay for the ticket. Dad wanted me to have fun. He wanted me to have teenager experiences. He just wished he could control those experiences, and make me stay a little girl forever.

The day of the concert was a total washout. Rain poured down for hours, and several of the first bands were canceled, but we went anyway. I met Nathan's four brothers, one of whom was an identical twin in our same class. All their older brothers looked exactly like them as well. It was fun to see a family that looked like they belonged together. The boys brought a blanket for us to sit on so we wouldn't get too muddy, and Nathan held me as we laughed, watched others dance, and enjoyed Primitive Radio Gods, The Wallflowers, and a dozen other bands. On the way home, Nathan kissed me and asked me to be his girlfriend. Thrilled that someone so nice and good-looking liked me, I said yes.

Between having Zac and his friends and Nathan and his friends, I settled into being the one girl of the bunch. Without sleepovers with girlfriends and only a limited amount of time I was allowed to spend with Nathan, I found myself with a considerable amount of free time, which I decided to dedicate to my schoolwork. I made it a goal to get straight As, and I was surprised at how easy it was, considering that in eighth grade I'd been failing almost every subject at different times, saved only by a move and fresh start in another town.

Rachel came to visit me over a four-day weekend, and I was shocked that her dad appreciated our friendship so much that he paid for a plane ticket. We had a blast. She met Zac, and we all went to Bell's Amusement Park in Tulsa to ride roller coasters. I felt like a real kid, doing kid things. I felt safe.

Dad wasn't working much, but I spent so much time at Grandma Rhodes's house and with Zac that I missed most of his outbursts. I was not surprised when he wanted to move back to the lake house in Graford, but I didn't want to go. I was finally building real relationships with my extended family, I was doing great in school, and I had a solid, respectable boyfriend. I asked my parents if I could live with my grandma, and they actually agreed with me that it would be a good idea. Grandma was reluctant at first because she didn't know if she could handle having a teenager in the house again, but she agreed that it had been nice getting to know me too.

Dad left me the Nissan Stanza, and they headed back to Possum Kingdom Lake.

My bedroom was now the room I had slept in when we stayed over for Christmas and Thanksgiving. My living room was the one I played cowboys and Indians in, and it was filled to the brim with happy photos of family. It was amazing to be in a place filled with memories and a sense of calm. I started going to church with Zac every Sunday, and I felt like I was home. Dad was an atheist and only spoke terribly about organized religion, but I discovered I loved going to church. The weekly positive messages, the community, and the feeling that everyone was just trying to do the right thing and help one another were things I could get behind.

Without any fighting or friction, life became peaceful and easy. I learned some of Grandma's recipes, laughed a lot with Zac, spent time with Nathan, and learned that I was related to almost everyone in Wagoner. I was so used to not knowing anyone and feeling isolated, scared, and alone. The only time I felt fear, shame, or doubt in Wagoner was when I got check-in calls from Dad. He would accuse me of something bad like taking advantage of Grandma, doing poorly in school, messing around with boys — it was always something, and it was rarely true, but instead of getting angry at Dad, I got defensive and sad. Grandma saw the tears every time I hung up. She hugged me and assured me that I was a good girl and that I was loved.

That's why it was so difficult when, at the end of the semester, Mom and Dad told me it was time to return to PK. I wanted to be with Rachel again, and I did miss my parents, but I'd also gotten used to not being afraid.

When I got back to our little house by the lake, it appeared that not much had changed, except that my flower beds were neglected, and all of my friends were partying even more than they did before. I was happy to be in the room I had decorated for myself and to be right down the street from

Rachel. I wrote letters to Grandma and to Nathan all the time, and Zac sent me mixed tapes. He'd always record himself saying something funny at the beginning.

The time I spent in Oklahoma with my grandma was the first time in my parent's marriage without any kids around. When I returned home, I learned that Mom and Dad considered filling their extra time in some unusual ways. Sipping her vodka and Squirt while puffing on a joint, Mom told me, "We've decided we either want to have another baby or become swingers." She fluttered through the pages of a printed catalog to show me other couples who were also looking to "have some fun." Deeply disturbed by either option, I still gave it some thought and recommended that if they must do one of those things, they opt out of having a baby. It's not that I wanted my parents to sleep with other people...yuck! I just thought it would be less detrimental, long term.

I have to assume their desire for distraction must have been extinguished by my presence in the house since there were no babies or new sexual partners, at least to my knowledge. Shortly after my return to PK, Michelle and Hailey moved back in with us too.

Michelle discovered that her friends in Virginia City weren't interested in hanging with a baby and that Jake wasn't interested in being a partner or a dad. He had broken into his mom's house to steal money for drugs and went to jail. To rebuild her life, Michelle moved back in with us and got a job at The Cliffs making good money. Hailey was now old enough to get into all my stuff. I loved her so much and would play and dance with her for hours, but I was also annoyed that I had no privacy.

For the rest of my junior and senior years, I worked hard at different restaurants around the lake, partied even harder, and focused on my schoolwork. After a falling-out with my two best friends, Lacy and Rachel, I spent more time with my basketball player boyfriend and his friends. This was a crowd that was going places — not to Harvard or Brown, but to college. Their version of partying was to have a couple of beers and talk about their futures, so I started thinking hard about what I wanted my future to look like.

Senior year, our one-act play did well in competitions. Thankfully, I mended my relationship with Lacy and Rachel, and we traveled all around the state, winning medals and moving up the ranks in our competitions. We didn't make it to state, but we went far, and we had an amazing experience together. When I was accepted to Tarleton State University with a scholarship for theater, I was excited and terrified. I'd chosen Tarleton because my friend Stacy was planning to go there, and at least then I wouldn't be alone when it was discovered I didn't belong. All my life, I'd honestly thought college was for attorneys, astronauts, and brain surgeons, not me. I cried — hard — many times, knowing that I was setting myself up to be seen, seen as poor, as stupid, as not pretty.

I received one theater scholarship for $2,000 a year, a $500 scholarship from the Cherokee Nation, and $250 from a local business. It wasn't much, but it was enough to give me the momentum I needed.

Dad saw my graduation as another opportunity to move, so he decided that it was time to go back to Virginia City, Nevada. He wouldn't let me stay in the house because he didn't trust me. He told me that I would go with them for the summer, and he promised to get me back to Texas in time for school. "Either that, or you can just take a year off to enjoy yourself, Steph," he offered.

I knew that most people in my situation who take a year off never end up going to college. I knew that you had to live in a state for at least a year to qualify for in-state tuition, and I knew that if I didn't start at Tarleton in the fall, I'd end up just like my parents.

Chapter 14

The closer we got to Virginia City, the more I feared that my best future would only exist in my rearview mirror. I was afraid that I'd somehow get stuck at the top of that mountain and never make my way back to Texas or the college that had accepted me against all odds. Adding to my dread was the prospect of spending my entire summer in a place where I no longer had any friends.

Arriving once again at the top of the mountain, we took up temporary residence in an old motel at the end of town. The parents of some of our friends owned the place, and the first day I arrived, my old friends Roxanne and Kali pulled up. I couldn't believe my luck. We were all surprised to see each other, and they invited me to a Tone Loc concert in Reno. Tone Loc didn't interest me, but it sounded more fun than hanging out with my parents in a stinky motel room, so we went and had a great time. When I got home, Michelle told me two cute guys were staying in a room across from us. One of her friends introduced us, and we instantly hit it off. Michelle was into Colt, and I was into Cody. My summer was looking up.

Within a week, we moved into what was the third apartment we lived in above Red's. Compared to the studio that all five of us shared when I was in the fourth grade, this one was enormous, with two stories and two bedrooms.

Rosalie was on my short list of people to reconnect with, and I found her working at a rock shop across the street from where Calamity Jane's used to be. She said she'd talk to Mike, the owner, but didn't think he had any work for me. My goal was to save money so that I didn't have to work much during school. Mike came back and said that he had no need for another cashier but that he had five potato sacks of petrified wood he'd collected that needed to be washed. If I didn't mind spending my days in the basement washing rocks, I had a job. Mike thought it would take a couple of months to complete the task, so I decided to make the best of spending my summer days in a basement.

To make cleaning the muck and mud off petrified wood fun, I jammed to music and found that I loved watching the clumps of nastiness transform into shiny, unique, beautiful specimens. After two weeks in the basement, though, I told Mike I was done — not because I quit, but because I had completed the job. He was surprised, and since I was such a good and happy worker, he found some more tasks for me to do. Organizing the storeroom and running inventory were right up my alley, especially since what I got to organize were crystals, precious stones, and beautiful fossils. I learned so much about these precious pieces of nature and became mesmerized by everything I touched. Since I was quick at that work, too, Mike found a position for me on the store floor. Working at a rock shop was not exactly a way to get rich, so I got a second job at The Mark Twain. Like Calamities, it was a bar at night and a hot dog and snack stand during the day. Staying the course and saving for school, I let nothing deter me from my goal.

Working seven days a week with double shifts doesn't quite lend itself to having a social life, but I somehow found a way. Michelle and I went out with Colt and Cody every night, frequenting the bars that Mom and Dad hung out in when we were kids. I was only seventeen, but no one seemed to care as long as I was dancing and drinking. Michelle quickly grew tired of Colt, but I was hooked on Cody. We had a wildly sensual relationship, having sex all over town.

While Dad never caught us, and I certainly never told him, Dad knew we were fooling around. He yelled at me more than ever, calling Colt and Cody Cort and Sport. Maybe he wanted to push me away so that he didn't have to feel the pain when I left. He knew I wasn't his baby anymore.

At Tarleton University, freshmen are invited to attend Duck Camp, a one-week camping trip in the summer where incoming students get to know one another. I had planned on returning to Texas in time to attend, but there were a few weeks between camp and move-in day at the dorms, and I didn't have a home close by to stay at in between.

Mom found a friend who had moved to Stephenville, where Tarleton was located. The friend said I could stay with them for free. Right. Settled...or not. All of a sudden, right before it was time for me to leave, we couldn't reach them. They didn't answer their phone, and Mom didn't know any other way to get in touch with them. To top it all off, Dad refused to help me leave Nevada, saying, "You have more money than I do, Steph, so you can figure it out." When I tried to explain that the saved money was so that I didn't need to work and worry while in school, he said there is a reason they call them starving students. That's the way it's supposed to be.

With no time for panic, I counted and calculated my money. I had just enough to get a one-way ticket to Dallas and stay in the cheapest roach motel in Stephenville until the dorms opened. I called and asked a friend in Possum Kingdom if she could pick me up from the airport, and she assured me that someone would be there.

On our last date, Colt took me to the Nevada State Fair, and then we said goodbye a few days later. Had I not had my eyes on college, I would have stayed with him. I wanted to make a life with him but knew that wasn't where I needed to be. There was a bigger life calling me, and I'd be damned if I was going to let either my father's resistance to letting me go or my own desire to stay with Colt get in the way of saying yes to that life.

Mom took me to the airport. We hugged and cried, and she handed me a letter and told me not to read it until I was on the plane. Settling into my seat, I unfolded the letter.

Dear Steph,

I want you to know how proud I am of you. I have no doubt you will be a success.

Love, Mom

When I landed in Dallas, my friend's dad picked me up — not exactly what I was expecting, but at least I had a ride. I stayed in our empty house on the lake for a few days, realizing for the first time ever just how expensive all the ingredients for a sandwich actually were when you're starting from nothing, and then packed everything I needed to move to college and headed to Stephenville. The same dad dropped me off...like literally dropped me and my bags on a corner on campus and left. It was only registration day for Duck Camp, but I'd brought everything I owned because I didn't have a car and I didn't have a place to live.

Luckily, a very nice young man named Jeremy could see that I was lost. He put all my things in the back of his truck, drove me across campus to check in, then drove me back to the dorms and carried my things to the front steps. He didn't ask for my number or try to be a creep. How refreshing it was to meet a genuinely good guy. Apparently, this is not an uncommon trait for Texas men.

After getting my things up the stairs and into the room I was only staying in for a night, I headed to the dining hall. As I walked through the line, I recognized someone in the kitchen. It was the husband of my mom's friend, who I was supposed to stay with. He saw me too, and we were both relieved to connect, but he told me that he and his wife no longer had room for me. From excitement to dread and reality in a matter of seconds, I thought back to the roach motel that was in my near future, but then I saw a lightbulb go off in his head, and he pulled me into the kitchen. "Do you remember Sharon?" he asked me, as he cornered her by the walk-in cooler. She had also worked with my mom at some point or another. He told Sharon my situation and asked if I could stay with her for a while. Put on the spot, she reluctantly said yes. When her shift ended, I handed all my extra things over to Sharon, and I went to Duck Camp the next day, knowing I'd have a bed to sleep in when I returned.

Duck Camp seemed great at first. There were about fifty cabins on the lake, with lots of activities for everyone to make new friends and memories. I'm a self-conscious redhead who looks like I don't have eyebrows without makeup on, so I didn't swim much, and I stayed fairly quiet and kept to myself. I watched to see who the popular girls were and what they were like, taking mental notes on what I needed to do to fit in.

Thankfully, Sharon was waiting for me when I got off the bus from camp, and she seemed much more excited to have me join her family for a little while.

As we chatted on the drive home, I realized just how much she was sacrificing for me. She lived in a very small trailer park a few blocks from campus. Her trailer had two bedrooms, and she had four kids, though her oldest daughter, who was sixteen, was living with a boy in town. Usually, her two middle kids shared a room, but she moved the boy into her room with the youngest. For my bed, she found a mattress from a trailer that someone had recently been evicted from, and I was to sleep on that in the room with her other daughter. Sharon's husband had recently been sent to prison, so she worked a few different jobs to keep things together.

After assuring her I would stay out of the way and not be an added expense, I quickly got a job at Sonic so that I could have one free meal and feed myself. I was extremely grateful for her hospitality and generosity, but her kids were in a different world. It was an insight into poverty that I hadn't seen before. The girls were very into boys, seeking attention from every male that came around and living like they were already adults. They stayed out all night with older men who had full-time jobs, and it was clear that they wanted to be wanted, wanted to be seen, and wanted to be taken care of. I wondered if that's what I looked like to others. Seeing young people run around town all hours of the night, smoking and drinking and looking for attention from the opposite sex was the beginning of my eyes opening to the world I had been living in.

On move-in day at Tarleton, parents unloaded cars full of new clothes and toiletries and groceries to help their kids start school as I took the few things I owned to my dorm. A customer from a restaurant I had worked at on the lake had gifted me a new comforter and sheets for graduation, so my room wasn't bare, but my parents didn't stock my mini fridge or take me out to one last dinner. I was now officially on my own as a college student. My friend Stacy, who'd convinced me to go to Tarleton with her, had decided not to attend college after all, but I knew that others from Graford would be on campus somewhere, and I had started fresh before. I wasn't afraid of making friends, but since this was college, I was certain that everyone would have more money than me and be smarter than me.

My first day of class settled my mind. I could see that I wasn't as out of my league as I'd feared. This small state school was for kids who came from working-class families who had graduated from small Texas high schools and were trying not to be the ones stuck in their small Texas town working at the local shop for the rest of their lives.

Being a young adult in Texas meant that I needed to learn how to two-step, so I called a guy who had graduated from Graford before I did and asked him to teach me. He was a student at Tarleton as well, and he agreed that two-stepping was an important part of my education. Craig Newman drove me in his pickup down a dirt road, put on his headlights, and taught me the steps. We giggled about how I needed to relax, and after a while, I let him lead. After two-step 101, we agreed that a dance floor would be a better place to continue my education, so he took me back to the dorm, and I never saw him again. He didn't try to kiss me or ask for my number. He simply did what I requested and left me alone.

In theater class, I auditioned for and got a role in the first main stage show, *One Flew Over the Cuckoo's Nest*. It was only a small role, but I was the first person to walk out on stage, which was terrifying. Rita, Forrest, and James had just transferred from other schools and were in the show with me. They all seemed so mature, good at their craft, and carried a presence like they were already stars on and off the stage.

Rehearsal was every weeknight, so there was no time to work during the day, and Sonic only paid minimum server wage, which was $3.25 an hour, plus the few little tips we got. So, I found a girl who was driving back and forth to the lake every weekend, and I got a job at The Cliffs where I could make $200-$400 a weekend and crash on a friend's couch while focusing on school during the week. And because The Cliffs was a golf course, restaurant, and deli, I could work triple shifts. If working triples sounds like a lot, I was also taking twenty-one hours my first semester. Working hard was what I knew, and it was the only part of my success I could control.

I eventually paid cash for a red Pontiac Fiero, which was super cute and sporty, though incredibly old and dangerous. The car was only in production for a few years before being taken off the market because they were made from fiberglass and crushed like paper when wrecked. I didn't know that when I purchased the car; I just liked that the headlights popped up when you turned them on.

With Mom, Dad, Michelle, and Hailey bouncing around the country, I went up to visit my grandma Rhodes and extended family in Wagoner every Thanksgiving. No matter what was happening in my life, being there always grounded me. I felt whole, loved, and proud. When I was a kid, Thanksgiving was the worst holiday of the year, but after moving out, it became my favorite.

That whole first semester was a whirlwind. I was constantly working and pushing myself to the brink, but it felt good. I felt like I could really do this...until I got a speeding ticket for going 100 miles per hour. The lake was an hour away from Stephenville, and the drive just seemed like a waste of time to me. I was doing everything I could to do all the things. For the most part, theater was my social life, although sometimes Lacy would drive down to take me out for a weekend. She was going to cosmetology school in Vernon, Texas, so she would drive three hours to pick me up, then we'd drive two hours to Fort Worth to go dancing at Southern Junction. I was super grateful for the two-stepping lessons I'd received because Texas dance halls are no joke! I'm not much of a country girl, but I do love to dance.

I survived my first year, and I only got one B each semester. Apparently, I was smart enough for college after all. My Bs were in PE.

By summer, my parents and Michelle had moved back to the lake. I assumed I would live with them for the summer and save money again, and again, I was wrong. Dad told me I needed to pay rent if I was going to live with them. It was only $300 a month, but I only had a bedroom that was eighty square feet, so it didn't quite seem fair, especially since Michelle never had to pay rent. It felt like I was getting punished for going off to college. I paid the rent money but told him I wouldn't live by his rules. I'd come and go as I pleased.

I partied and worked hard all summer, but I was ready to get back to school when the fall semester started. Rita and Forrest and I got close quickly at the beginning of that year. Forrest moved to Florida for work and asked if I would live with Rita so that she wouldn't be alone. He said it would be rent-free. I'd already paid for the semester in the dorm, but I knew I couldn't refuse a free opportunity to live off-campus with my idol, Rita.

When she offered me a role in the workshop show she was directing, it was an easy yes. *Where Have All the Lightning Bugs Gone* is a beautiful one-act play that is full of wonder, imagination, and romance. It was a dream role for me, and I was cast with a very handsome man named Trey. It's a two-person show, so when he asked me to run lines together, I assumed he just wanted to rehearse. We met in Rita's apartment, and it quickly became clear he wasn't interested in the script. Trey was five years older than me, very well-built, funny, and charming. I was all in. Between the wonder of the play and his wonder for me, I fell for him. It was obvious we were going to get married, have beautiful children, and travel the world together. I even took him home to meet my parents...who hated him.

Still commuting back and forth to The Cliffs, I fell asleep one Monday morning while driving home. I woke up when the wheels hit the gravel and instantly realized I was about to go off a cliff. I jerked the wheel in the other direction and flipped the car. Everything was in slow motion, and somehow I knew I wasn't going to die, but I was so mad at myself. How was I going to continue to work and go to school? Dang it, I'm so stupid! After coming to a stop upside down on the other side of the road, I released the seatbelt and climbed out of the car feetfirst. A truck had already stopped. An older gentleman was in tears and ran up to hug me and ask if I was okay. He said he thought I was dead because all he saw when he pulled up was two tiny legs sticking out of a flat car. He hugged me again tightly as if I were his own daughter.

Just then, a police car pulled up and asked what had happened. He asked the man, not me. In fact, he never even acknowledged me until the man pointed out that he didn't know me and was only there to help. The officer gave me a speeding ticket and called a tow truck. He continued to talk to the man and told him where the tow truck would take my car. This was the part of small-town Texas I didn't like. Of course, the young girl was not worth talking to, not smart enough to take care of herself. After the officer left, the man apologized for the officer's actions and drove me to Stephenville. This was the part of Texas that I loved.

Back at the apartment, I started to wonder if college was too much for me. I thought about how every other kid gets care packages, money in the mail, stocked refrigerators, and dinners out with family. I wondered why everything was pulling me back. How it would have been so much easier to do what I had always done, to live the way my parents lived.

That week at school, I felt deflated and afraid and was too scared to tell Trey and my dad that I had wrecked my car. The last thing I needed was to be lectured or disappoint anyone more than I'd already disappointed myself. I told Rita I didn't know how I was going to get back and forth to work, and she said if I could get her a job there, she could drive us both.

Wow! That was easy; now, onto telling Trey.

Used to being either berated or dismissed by the men in my life, I was sure he'd yell at me and tell me I was an idiot, but instead, he was concerned about me and happy that I was okay. With a little more confidence, I called and told Dad, and though he wasn't quite as gentle, he was glad I was safe.

This response might seem like an obvious one to expect, but it's not one I'd frequently received from my dad.

Eventually, I got several of my theater friends to work at The Cliffs, which made my commute much simpler and a bit more fun. The Cliffs would give me a room for the weekend if there was one, and if not, there were plenty of floors and couches to crash on.

Mom, Dad, Michelle, and Hailey moved to Pensacola, Florida, and worked to sell the house at the lake. When I told Dad he should keep it and rent it out, he yelled at me and told me I was a selfish bitch like his sister (whom he blamed for his mother's death) and just wanted it for myself. I was honestly just thinking it would be the smartest retirement option. They could either earn rental income or live rent-free. Seemed like a no-brainer to me, but Dad didn't like hearing advice from his college idiot daughter.

At the end of my sophomore year, Trey decided to move to Austin. I don't think he was much of a college student anyway. He was an ROTC guy and trying to do what he could to make that work, but his family had money, and he didn't feel that college was the path for him. On my very first trip to Austin, I knew it was a place I wanted to live too. It was time for a bigger city and a bigger school and to be around people whose ideals aligned with mine, which is to say, more liberal than rural Texas. My vision of a happy life with Trey quickly progressed when he asked me to move into his Austin apartment with him. He told me he loved me, and we wrote poetry to each other and did all the silly things young people in love do, like gaze into each other's eyes for hours without saying much of anything.

However, the reality was that I needed to save up some money before moving to Austin, so I decided to spend one last summer with my parents. By then, they had moved to Gulf Shores, Alabama. My plan was to work all summer to save for a car, then drive back to Texas and live happily ever after. I'd already proven I had the strength and momentum to dip back into their lives and find my way out again, and now I knew my best future was still in front of me.

Chapter 15

Hard work and an unwavering focus, laced with sporadic dashes of good fortune, seemed to be my recipe for getting ahead. At least I could control two out of three.

In Gulf Shores, BJ's Seafood Restaurant offered me both lunch and dinner shifts, in addition to bookkeeping and errands, and I said yes to all of it. My only goal that summer was to save up enough money to buy a car that would get me around once I got to Austin. Outside of work, I still managed to go to the beach here and there, run in the mornings, and do some Tae Bo workouts, but I wasn't there to make friends or party; this was just an extended layover.

Living back home, however, had its challenges. It was during this time that Dad and I had a cataclysmic blowout. It ended with me screaming, "I love no one more on this earth than you, and you hurt me more than anyone on this planet ever could." It started with me saying how amazing it was to watch Hailey come into her own, that she was starting to become aware of herself. Dad immediately jumped into a screaming rant about me psychoanalyzing her and that I was really just a stupid, selfish bitch who thought I was better than anyone else. The fight went on for about thirty minutes before I realized Hailey was watching the whole thing. I wanted to throw something at him; I honestly wanted to kill him. I wanted him to go away and never hurt anyone again. Instead, I went inside and sat with Hailey, who tried to comfort me and justify my dad's behavior. She reminded me of myself, which made me even sadder.

Over the summer, my earnings afforded me a red Chevy Cavalier and a plane ticket for Trey to come to Gulf Shores and drive back with me. We'd been talking on the phone all summer, but I was dying to see him in person and finally start our new life together. Just a few weeks before he was set to fly out, he delivered some unexpected news. Turns out he'd been cheating on me...for the entire summer. Hearing this was like getting the wind knocked out of my chest, and what's worse is he didn't even seem sorry.

Although Dad suggested it, staying in Pensacola was never an option I considered. But now that I wasn't going to live happily ever after with Trey, I needed a new plan. I'd been expecting a romantic trip halfway across the country and a move into the city of my dreams with the man of my dreams. Instead, I was going to go to Austin by myself. I went to see the Blue Angels by myself and then drove almost 700 miles alone. It was like every great romantic comedy, except we didn't end up together in the end. I rolled the windows down and let my hair blow, blasting and singing Cindy Lauper's "True Colors" and "Time After Time" along with other power ballads. I danced in my seat, I cried a lot, and I made my way back to Texas.

I was bound and determined to make it on my own. So much so that I was willing to live out of my car, but Dad came to the rescue. He knew a family who lived in Taylor, which is just outside of Austin — a couple he'd met many years ago when he lived in Colorado sometime during the '70s. Apparently, they hadn't talked much since then, but Dad still had their number, and he told them his crazy daughter needed a place to stay. Diann and John knew Dad because his second wife was Diann's best friend. They knew him as a wild alcoholic who lost his temper often, and somehow, they still agreed to let his daughter move into their home.

When I was about an hour away from Taylor, Texas, I called Diann. I hadn't even heard my dad talk about them before, and the first conversation I had with Diann was her telling me that the back door was unlocked and that I was to go in and make myself at home. Their oldest son, Jared, was away at the University of Texas, so I could use his room at the end of the hallway. Their two other sons would be home from high school in a few hours. Now that is trust!

I pulled up to their perfect white house in the country, let myself in, and brought the few suitcases of clothes I had with me to the back bedroom. The quaint and beautiful home had wood floors in every room and bookshelves lining every wall filled with well-worn books and family photos. It was clean and comfortable.

When Chris and Sam came home from school, they took me for a drive around the property. They had 300 acres that went from the creek to the road. They shared the land with John's sister Carol who lived with their grandma in a house their grandpa had built when he purchased the land. When Diann came home, she made dinner for all of us, and I told them I promised I'd be out of their hair as soon as I could. They told me to take my time and do what I needed to do, but the next day, I drove to Austin and started looking for a job.

A girl I had met from Tarleton was also moving to Austin, so we planned to get an apartment together. Finding something we could afford was a challenge, but I located a cool Austin-y place on Montopolis for only $800 a month for a two-bedroom, and within a few weeks, I had a job at Al Capone's Italian Restaurant on Riverside Drive.

Our apartment wasn't going to be available for a few months, so I drove an hour from Taylor to Austin almost every day to work and take classes. I enrolled in Austin Community College to take some more core classes and applied to Southwest Texas State University for the next year. Applying to the University of Texas had been my original goal, but most of my credit hours wouldn't have transferred, and I couldn't afford to backtrack.

Driving back and forth between Taylor and Austin was exhausting. Sometimes I'd nap in my car or at Zilker Park, but the peace and comfort I felt living with the Foxes were worth it. They took me in, no questions asked, and made me feel like a part of the family. It was a generosity that made a deep impression on me, and while they were the kind of people who'd help anyone without thinking twice, their kindness instilled in me a lasting sense of belonging that I carry with me now.

Another reason I didn't mind my commute to Austin on weekends was there was a super cute guy who played drums at the restaurant during my shift. His name was Matthew, and he looked like a nice guy — the kind that went to church and came from a good family, so I was certain he wouldn't be into me, but the piano player told me that Matthew thought I was cute. Like kids passing notes in class, I told the piano player I thought Matthew was cute, so we found a day to go on a date.

Our first date was his birthday, which happened to fall on Labor Day weekend. I didn't know it was his birthday until we were there. He said it was just a convenient day because we were both off work. We were supposed to meet at a coffee shop, but it was closed for the holiday, so we ended up going to Chili's. We were comfortable together from the very beginning, so we hung out all day. It seemed easy, not like anything I'd ever experienced before. He'd moved to Austin from Louisiana to play music, and from what I could tell, he was going places.

Saying goodbye to the Foxes, I moved into the Metropolis apartments with Mary Ann, where we lived for a year as I continued working and taking classes. In addition to my regular job at Al Capone's, I picked up banquet shifts at Shoreline Grill, a high-end restaurant that also hosted large events. I auditioned and got a role in a Shakespeare play, which was terribly done, but I was happy to be performing.

Matthew picked up gigs with bands, and I attended every one of his shows I could. We were young and working hard to get our start, as individuals and together.

When people imagine a young musician, they usually think of torn jeans, long hair, and a rock-and-roll lifestyle, but that wasn't Matthew at all. He had a good day job, didn't drink much, never tried drugs, and hated smoking. Though I had tried to quit smoking several times since I was seventeen, it always crept back into my life. It was kind of a support blanket for me. That is until Matthew told me he didn't want to kiss me if I had been smoking. Somehow, quitting became much easier.

On the radio, I heard about an acting audition for Best New Talent of the Year. The winner would be sent to Los Angeles to compete and possibly be scouted. It was a long shot, but I thought I'd give it a try. I performed a monologue I thought would help a small redhead from Texas stand out. With a queen's accent, lots of hand gestures, and a bit of sassy hip action, this one was bound to bring laughs. Think Marisa Tomei in *My Cousin Vinny,* performed by Amy Adams. The winning contestants would be flown to Los Angeles from all around the country, and somehow I was one of five selected from Austin! I asked one of my Tarleton buddies if she could go with me, but it didn't work out for her, so I asked Matthew to come along. I thought he would enjoy LA, and it would be our first trip together. He excitedly accepted, got his own plane ticket, and we made the trek.

Apparently, there was a famous LA drummer who agreed to give Matthew a lesson while he was in town. It was very exciting for both of us!

The format of the competition was for contestants to audition again by their age group in front of a small panel of judges, and three people from each age group would be selected to perform in front of a large audience that was filled with producers, casting directors, and other scouts.

My first audition went fine, but I was shaky. I was pretty certain I didn't make it, but I was still happy for the opportunity and the adventure. At six o'clock that evening, all the contestants were brought to the ballroom and called onto the stage by age group. It reminded me of *Star Search* and all the times I had watched through the windows from the playground in Carson City. When my age group was called up, we stood like cattle, and the first name they called was Stephanie Mallory. I stared blankly ahead until the girl next to me nudged me and said, "Isn't that you? Aren't you Stephanie Mallory?" Oh God, that is my name! I walked off stage as they called two other names and walked right back on to perform my monologue in front of a huge audience.

The lights were bright, but it didn't matter. I couldn't see anything anyway. All I could see was black. I put on my sass and pulled out my humor, and hoped to God that the words coming out of my mouth made any sense at all; then I walked off the stage and took what seemed like my first breath. They called the second runner-up first, and again they called Stephanie Mallory. I didn't win the competition, but I placed! In a talent search across the United States, I placed. The winner was fantastic, and I was happy for her.

When the show was over, I ran into the audience looking for Matthew, but he wasn't there. I looked in the hall, but he wasn't there either. I found him in the hotel room watching TV. He said his lesson fell through, and he didn't feel like leaving the room. I was sad for him but told him we needed to go out and celebrate. I had done well. I was the second runner-up. After some cajoling, we went to a very quiet steak dinner at a chain restaurant, and then we flew home the next day. I was not sure how to feel. I performed well and was recognized, but I wanted to honor Matthew's sadness for not getting what he had hoped from the trip. I didn't realize it until years later but I was so used to putting everyone else first that it didn't occur to me that he should have put his feelings aside to celebrate my accomplishment and explore LA with me.

Though life was still life with its imperfect moments, overall everything was going really well. I was making decent money, I had a stable boyfriend, and I was still working toward my degree. In fact, I sold the Cavalier and purchased a brand-new Honda Civic. I went to the dealership by myself, wrote the first check, and drove off the lot as a more confident person. My parents had never owned a new car. They would never have qualified, and here I was, twenty years old with a brand-new car. Sure, it came with a monthly payment, but I was doing all right.

Unfortunately, working two jobs is great for paying rent and getting a new car but not so good for financial aid. When I found out that I no longer qualified for assistance, I was devastated. I had done everything right. I had worked my ass off to provide for myself without any help from my parents or anyone else and was being penalized because, for the first time in my life, I wasn't poor...enough!

Sitting out a semester to save more money meant I risked dropping out and being a waitress forever. Crushed by this thought, I cried as Matthew held me and assured me that everything was going to be alright. It would only be a few short months before I'd start at Southwest Texas, and I could apply for loans instead of grants. The payments would be deferred until after graduation, so I wouldn't need to worry about it. He was calm, steady, and exactly what I needed.

After my lease at Metropolis was up, I moved in with some other friends from Tarleton who graduated and moved to Austin. We lived in a beautiful two-story, four-bedroom house in North Austin, and I continued working at Shoreline Grill. It was better and easier money than Al Capone's, and a lot of the income was undeclared cash tips. Having just one job that afforded me a nice place to live made it clear why dropping out would have been the easier path, but I wouldn't let myself get close to the edge of that slippery slope. Growing up, I'd seen first-hand what life looks like when just getting by is your biggest goal. I wanted more for myself.

Chapter 16

By Christmastime, my parents had moved back to Gulf Shores, Alabama, and for the life of me, I can't remember where they had gone to and come back from. The longer I lived on my own and became more stable, the harder I had to try to keep up with their address changes. But since they were far away, Matthew asked if I wanted to go home with him for the holidays. This was the first time a guy ever officially introduced me to his parents. Yes, I wanted to go, but I was scared. I was always scared that people would see me for the poor girl I really was. The girl who works hard and finds luck but isn't quite smart enough. I'd met his mother, Rosemary, once before when she came into the restaurant while visiting Matthew. She even bought me a gift, so I knew she was nice, but they seemed rich, or richer than anyone I knew. I joked that I was going to show up to the Christmas tree in footie pajamas, and with a very serious face, he told me not to. He said his family was very formal, and everyone gets fully dressed before going to the tree. I'm sure I lost all the color in my face before Matthew told me he was kidding. He was always joking, and I always fell for it.

In spite of my anxiety, Christmas was delightful! I met his Italian grandma from Queens, whose name was actually Santa. She made sure my tummy was full...of spaghetti and wine. I also got to meet his brother,

Scott, his stepdad, Hardy, and then his dad and stepmom, Lawrence and Debbie, the next day. They were all kind, funny, and inviting. I felt at home with them, and I fell even more in love with Matthew for sharing them with me, and me with them.

What must it have been like growing up in a family like that! How had Matthew and I come from such different families and formative experiences and still managed to arrive at a single point of connection? It didn't matter that he'd had money and consistency and support while my foundation had been in constant flux; we were made for each other.

Some people would consider it strange that I didn't take the day off work on my twenty-first birthday, but I wasn't planning to celebrate. I was going to work a double shift and go relax with Matthew. On my way to Shoreline that morning, I tuned into 101X on the radio, and they started talking about people jumping out of skyscrapers in New York City. There was something about an airplane and a fire. I looked around at other drivers and realized everyone was hearing the same thing. A heavy feeling filled us all at the same time as we struggled to wrap our heads around the news.

When I got to work, the news was playing instead of music, and we all learned what was happening as it happened. The event we were supposed to work that day was canceled, so we all sat around and talked for a while. One of the waiters was a political science major at the University of Texas, so he explained the background and who was likely responsible, but no amount of background info could really explain why or how something like this was really happening. It was just too horrific to fully comprehend. Then someone looked over at me and said, "Oh shit, Stephanie, isn't it your birthday today?"

Leaving Shoreline early, I went to Matthew's apartment, and we watched the television like zombies as the world tried to understand the horror unfolding. Matthew didn't mention my birthday, and I didn't care. There were more important things to think about that day. Matthew had family who lived in Manhattan, and thank goodness they were safe, but the same couldn't be said for some of their friends.

From that day on, life was different for everyone, but we had to keep moving. We had bills to pay and lives to live. I developed an obsession with the news and, with it, a fear — a new kind of fear — not a terror of what might happen inside my home, but what could happen out in the world. As the country rolled into war, nightmares dominated my sleep, and I assumed I wasn't the only one.

Slowly, planes started flying again, and everyone who could go back to work did. I started planning for college life at Southwest Texas State University and took a trip to San Marcos to visit the theater department. The call board posted notices for upcoming shows, and I also found a post for a room for rent for one hundred dollars a month. Done. I called the number, and the guy on the other side asked me if I was cool. "Sure, I'm cool," I said. He told me that he was gay and the other roommate was a porn star. I didn't expect the porn star thing, but he said she keeps it out of the house, and she keeps to herself. We just wouldn't be able to talk about it at school because it's kind of a secret. I'm good at keeping secrets, especially for cheap rent.

I moved from the big, beautiful house I shared with my Tarelton friends to a three-bedroom duplex that smelled like pot and cat urine. My room was hardly bigger than a closet, but it was large enough to fit a twin bed and a dresser, and I was happy there. I didn't have to work much at all. I even discovered the joy of napping! To make some extra cash, I got a part-time job at the college bookstore, which I loved for about a month, but after everyone had purchased their textbooks and the store was deserted, I couldn't take it. I needed something more fast-paced, so I went back to Shoreline and worked events on the weekends.

School started, and auditions for *Death of a Salesman* were on the first day. I nailed the audition, even though I had a headache of the century, and got a role in another main stage show. After watching my performance, Matthew told me he loved me, and I knew I loved him back. The school year flew by. I made friends with people in the cast but didn't hang out with anyone because I was working in Austin and dating Matthew. Matthew joined a talented band called Jefferson Truitt, which was a huge win for him, and it felt like we were both making strides in a good direction.

When my lease was up, I agreed to get an apartment with some of the cast members. The lease would start at the beginning of the school year, but my duplex lease was up when school ended, so I asked Matthew if I could live with him for the summer. He and his roommate reluctantly agreed. I stayed in his room most of the time. He had a twin mattress that we put on the floor every night for me to sleep on, then we put it back in the closet every morning. He was a light sleeper, so he preferred I didn't sleep on his bed. While I was living with Matthew, he overheard my conversations with my parents and saw my tears after the calls ended. He taught me that the way they communicated with me was not okay. That someone I love, and who says they love me, should never say the things my parents said to me. I liked living with Matthew. We got along well, but it was clear he didn't want me in his space. Shoreline Grill was slow, so I was almost always home when he got off work. I tried to meet him at the door with kisses, but he asked me to give him a little space.

We were both happy when it came time for me to move out. I purchased a full-size bed and a bedspread I thought he'd like, but when I invited him over to my new apartment to see it, he broke up with me. No real reason; I didn't ask. I didn't push back because if someone wants to break up with you, then you let them, right?

Losing Matthew after we'd been so happy together, and after meeting his family, just didn't make sense to me. I cried every day. I tried to go on dates, but it felt terrible, like I was cheating on him even though he had broken up with me. I tried to explain all this to one of my roommates, and we began to tell stories about our childhood.

I told her about how I had lost my virginity when I was twelve. As mentioned earlier, this was not something I felt ashamed about when it happened, but the judgment I'd received when I shared my experience made me feel ashamed. I'd lost my childhood friends over it, and it was clear by other people's reactions that what I'd done wasn't okay. But when I started sharing the story this time, an interesting thing happened. I started by telling her about sledding, and she got really into the story. She had never seen snow before, so I got excited telling her about the day and how fun it was, and I realized that I could change the way I felt about what had happened. I didn't need to feel sad, ashamed, or mad about the experience. I could feel happiness knowing I chose it. I could forgive him... and forgive myself.

That led me to think about forgiveness of past deeds, and I decided that my birth father should know that I was doing okay. I wanted him to be proud of me. I asked Mom if she knew how to get in touch with him, and she got me a phone number for an aunt she used to keep in touch with. I opened a bottle of wine, and after that, I dialed the number, which opened a brand new can of worms. The aunt was happy to hear from me, but instead of asking about my life, she proceeded to tell me every bad thing my father had ever done or been accused of. It was gut-wrenching to hear that my biological father had done so many monstrous things. By the end of the conversation, I had finished the bottle of wine and fell into a puddle of tears. How could I come from something so terrible? In contrast, I was grateful for the dad who chose to raise me. He had his faults, but he was better than the alternative.

Going to therapy was the next step on my path to healing, although when I began, I had no idea how much I would uncover. It was like digging up my past and spreading the contents of my life all over the floor to be examined more closely. There it was, staring back at me — the loss, the fear, the anger, and all the coping mechanisms I'd used to get by all those years. It was messy, and the counselor was dumbfounded that I could tell so many traumatic stories and laugh instead of cry.

Moving out of my parent's home and starting college was the beginning of me seeing my life through a new lens. This lens made me angry about everything I had missed, the names I had been called that stuck with me like curses, and the anchor that kept pulling me back down to start over again and again. Therapy was the magnifying glass that allowed me to begin to heal. The storm clouds of anger went away as I remembered the love my parents had for me, and I saw that they were struggling with their own curses. I learned new ways of processing my past and my present experiences, and I quickly assimilated those tools into my life.

Still, I couldn't stop thinking about Matthew, so I called and asked him to help me with an audition. It was my senior year of college, and I had never auditioned for a musical. We were about to do *Chicago,* and even though I'm a terrible singer and haven't done any choreographed dance since I left Mesquite in the middle of eighth grade, I knew this was my last chance. He picked out some music and let me borrow it. That was my in.

My audition was absolutely terrible. I almost kicked someone in the face doing a turn kick, so I didn't even bother to check the call board, but I was proud that I had tried. I returned the CD to Matthew, and he told me he was moving — not out of Austin but downtown. He had found a one-bedroom apartment, and he wanted me to see it. It was tiny, but it was perfect for him. He could walk to get ice cream and to sandwich shops, and it was close to the Austin scene but in a quiet little space that was all his. I asked him to attend an event with me, and after that, he asked if I would go on a date with him for Valentine's Day. After spending a little more time together, he told me he wanted to be together again. So did I.

I didn't focus much on why Matthew had broken up with me in the first place. He said it just seemed to him like we were either needing to take it to the next level or break up. He wasn't ready for marriage, and he felt like he needed a little space, so breaking up seemed like the right option for him at the time.

Back in our groove, Matthew was picking up gigs from a guy named Mike Mortichi. Mike placed musicians all over town, so Matthew got to play with the Austin Symphony Orchestra, Riverbend Church, and even Ray Charles. It was amazing! I loved watching his bands play and often went by myself and found friends amongst the crowd. I went to every show I could as long as it was an hour or less away.

Meanwhile, I performed in several small productions, and each time, Matthew asked me if it was important for him to watch. I told him no. They were just small productions. If he didn't want to come, he didn't have to. He didn't care for plays, so he didn't come.

With graduation fast approaching, an opportunity of a lifetime presented itself. A handful of students would be selected to study with the Royal Shakespeare Academy in Stratford-upon-Avon, England. I didn't know how I would be able to afford it, but I knew I had to try, and as luck would have it, I was accepted. To make the most out of our time in England, those of us who'd been accepted attended classes on campus to learn as much as we could about the man, the time, the plays, the sonnets, everything!

Mom, Dad, Michelle, and Hailey were still in Gulf Shores, and when I asked if they were going to make it to graduation, Mom told me I needed to find them a place to live. Surprised but not surprised by their inability to just take a trip, I waited for the Sunday Austin paper so I could send them some rental options. When I called to tell Mom that I had mailed the paper, she said it was too late. They were already packing and were leaving the next day. They needed to have a place within two days. I was looking forward to having them close, but I didn't want them too close, so since I loved living in South Austin, I looked in Georgetown (which is on the far north side of Austin). I found them a small apartment that they were able to get into within a few weeks, and in the meantime, they lived in a motel. Some things never change.

Only a few days before I was booked to fly to England, I received a panic-filled call from Michelle. She said that Mom was bleeding from her head and was on the way to the hospital in an ambulance. She said Mom didn't fall, so I was really confused but also very scared. After calling into work, I headed straight for Brackenridge Hospital.

When I arrived, Michelle and Dad still couldn't explain what had happened. Dad said they had had a great day. They went out to lunch together. She read her book for a little while, and she was doing her puzzle. They were so very relaxed. And then suddenly, she just got really flush and went to lie down. He thought she had a migraine, so he went to get her a cold washcloth. As far as I knew, he had never taken care of my mom, so I knew he was scared. He said he could tell very quickly that something wasn't right and called 911. It was clear to the paramedics that Mom needed to go to a larger hospital in Austin, rather than the local one.

After waiting for what seemed like way too long, two surgeons entered the room and told us that my mother had suffered an aneurysm. They began to explain to my dad what that meant and what needed to happen next, but he quickly stopped them. He said, "I don't understand; you're going to have to talk to Stephanie." They explained to me that a blood vessel had burst in her brain, and they needed to perform surgery immediately. There were two options for surgery, and we were going to need to choose — I was going to have to choose. One option was newer and involved a scope that would enter through her armpit. The other was tried and true and involved cutting my mom's skull open. I looked at my dad, and he told me I was going to make the decision because he couldn't. I knew that every moment the doctors stood there talking to me, the swelling and bleeding were increasing, so I asked as many questions as I could before making what felt like a snap decision. Of course, I didn't want my mom's skull to be cut open, but the surgeon said they had a lot more experience with that procedure, and the chance of infection was lower, so that's the option I chose. They told me that either way, we needed to prepare ourselves. Most people do not survive brain aneurysms.

I hugged Michelle and Dad and told them everything was going to be okay, and then I realized that I needed to call my aunts. I had grown close to Zac's mom when I lived there, so I called Aunt Virginia first. I was doing so well being strong, but as soon as I heard her voice, I couldn't breathe. I managed to share the news in short bursts, through tears and hyperventilation, as I slumped down on the floor. I couldn't get it all out at the time, but it was enough to say that Mom was in the hospital and may not come out alive.

Knowing that Mom wanted to be cremated, I kept imagining her body being burned. I wasn't ready. We paced the floors for hours. No one ate or said anything. I eventually calmed down enough to call my uncle Don and tell him the full story. He asked if they needed to come, and I told him I didn't know.

A billion hours went by before a surgeon came back to tell us Mom had made it through surgery and was resting. She'd be in ICU for a while, so we should go home and rest. We'd be able to see her in the morning. I called Aunt Virginia and told her the good news, then drove to my apartment in complete disbelief.

On my way home from the hospital, it hit me that I shouldn't go to England. Who could focus on studying at the Royal Shakespeare Academy when I needed to take care of Mom? The following day, I went back to the hospital as soon as I woke up. Mom was on some serious painkillers but woke up enough to tell me that she would be okay. She didn't want me to miss out on a chance of a lifetime, and she wouldn't be mad if something happened to her while I was gone. "Steph, I'll be mad if you *don't* go," she insisted weakly and assured me she was strong enough to get through this. She said she'd be okay, and for some reason, I believed her.

Two days later, with my mom still in intensive care, I touched down in London. I didn't have to deny my past to stop being defined by it. I'd become the girl who works hard, finds luck, and is smart enough to be selected into a prestigious program.

Chapter 17

I called Mom from England as often as I could, but as a very poor college student, I could hardly afford a sandwich, much less multiple international calls. Fortunately, we stayed at a bed and breakfast, which meant at least one full meal a day would be covered, and I loved the English breakfast they served with eggs, roasted tomato, sausage, beans, mushrooms, and English bacon — which resembles American ham.

Knowing my mom was getting better and in good care, I let myself become deeply immersed in the experience with the Royal Shakespeare Academy. As a group, we spent our days taking classes on every topic of Shakespeare's works and were granted access to the basement, which was a library that held his original works. We visited his childhood home and strolled through the gardens that inspired him. Oh, the gardens were a dream — so lush and beautiful. We attended exquisite performances at the Royal Shakespeare Theatre, The Swan, and The Globe. We even got to sit in the pub and chat with the actors a few times.

On an off weekend, I traveled to Edinburgh, Scotland, with another student named William. It was an easy train ticket, and we stayed in a fifteen-dollar hostel. William took a nap there, but I didn't want to sleep at all. I walked the streets, toured the castle, and chatted with locals. The sun never actually went down, so William met me out at a pub, and we took in the spirit of the city. We only had one night there, so I slept on the train on the way back to Stratford.

The whole experience was phenomenal and worth every bit of penny-pinching and life-stretching. In another life, I could have stayed there forever, but I needed to get back to check on my mom, and I wanted to get back to Matthew.

After her aneurysm, Mom quit smoking. Her doctor told her that she would heal faster if she quit, so she got hypnotized. She tried to convince Michelle and Dad to quit, but they didn't have any interest. It was the first time Mom took an active interest in living a healthier life, and while I wasn't sure her fervor would last, it was nice to see the effort.

Once I was home and assured that Mom was okay, I reflected on my trip, and I realized for the first time that I was capable of having really big, expansive experiences outside of what I knew and what I expected of my life. It was the first time that I realized that life could expand beyond my wildest dreams. And my dreams were just the beginning, the indicators that would light the way to more possibilities than I could see from my current vantage point.

On graduation day, several of my family members and friends attended. Matthew was there, Michelle, Mom, Dad, and Hailey were there, of course, The Foxes, some aunts and uncles, and my sweet Grandma Rhodes. They drove down from all over the country to watch me walk the stage, and I could see that they were all proud of me. I had worked so hard for that singular moment. I had proven to myself and the world that I could do it. I could cross the chasm.

I let myself revel in my accomplishment for about twenty-four hours before switching from student mode into career mode. I went to school so that I wouldn't have to be a waitress for the rest of my life. My roommates and several of my classmates were moving to Chicago and New York to make their mark, but I didn't want to continue to be a starving artist, and I also didn't want to leave Matthew, so I started looking around for a job in Austin.

I wasn't having much luck. Apparently, a theater degree doesn't provide much of a future in anything other than call center work. I was still sure I needed to move on, though, so I told the owner of Shoreline Grill that I was looking for a real job. He smiled and told me that the consultant they recently hired recommended me for a new position he was creating, Director of Sales and Marketing. He asked if I'd be interested, and I immediately accepted.

When I enrolled in college, marketing was my declared major, but with acting scholarships and my passion for theater, I never took one class. Oh gosh, I wish I had. I immediately went to the bookstore and purchased everything that looked like it would be helpful. I attended every sales or marketing seminar I could, and I dove in the best way I knew how...headfirst.

The position covered all marketing efforts and also sales and coordination of events. It was fun being on the other side of the clipboard. I purchased suit dresses and nice shoes, got myself a one-bedroom apartment in a fourplex, and purchased brand-new matching living room furniture. I had arrived!

For my birthday, Matthew got me a cat. She was an adorable and feisty orange tabby. I wanted to name her Foofer, but everyone told me that was dumb, so she decided on the name Zoey. Zoey made a habit of sleeping on my chest for a while each night before terrorizing the house while I slept. When the landlord refused to fix a gas leak under the water heater, Zoey and I found a decent one-bedroom apartment on South First Street.

While I was becoming a career woman, Matthew decided to go back to school to get his master's degree in music. His undergrad was in music, and though playing random gigs around town was fun, and he liked teaching lessons to high school students, he felt like he needed to do more. Hanging out with him during that time usually consisted of my cleaning his kitchen, cooking, cleaning again, then leaving to let him study. We existed this way for months on end, and while I knew I still loved him, I didn't love how little I was getting from him in return.

I wanted more from our relationship, and I wanted more from my career. Though working at Shoreline was a great experience, I still wanted to get out of the restaurant industry. I called and met with a few marketing agency owners to see how I could work my way in but was turned down due to having the wrong college degree, lack of experience, and lack of a definable talent. I was feeling a bit lost and like I needed a big change. I considered moving to Las Vegas to be an event coordinator there. At least I would be working with exciting events in an exciting town. Untethered from work, my relationship, and my family...I could have gone anywhere.

After months of feeling detached from Matthew, I made the decision it was time to let him go. I knew we had the potential to be great together, but it would require both people in the relationship to be equally invested. I was tired of holding my breath. When I told Matthew we had lost touch and that it felt like he wanted to break up with me, he sat me on his lap and told me he was sorry for being so distant. He told me to find the nicest restaurant in town, and he would take me there.

It wasn't difficult to find the nicest restaurant in town. It was the sister restaurant to Shoreline called Jeffrey's. I officed across the hall from Jeffrey and told him Matthew's request, and he said he'd take care of the reservation. During dinner, Matthew and I chatted like we normally did, but then he got serious. He held my hand and told me he couldn't imagine spending the rest of his life with anyone else. I felt the same. We talked about getting married in the future, and since we had already been together for five years, it seemed right that we would stay together.

With the future-husband box checked off my list of life to-dos, I started thinking about owning a home. I wanted to live somewhere long enough to see my seeds grow into flowers. I wanted to know that it was mine. I told Matthew I was thinking about buying a house but couldn't afford to pay a mortgage on my own, so I asked if he wanted to move in with me or if I should start looking for a roommate. Scared but happy, he decided to purchase the house with me. Through networking, I found a real estate agent and mortgage broker, and I started the process. In the meantime, I drove around neighborhoods imagining myself owning one of the beautiful homes in Austin as motivation to sell more, so I could make more commission and secure a house that we love.

As we toured homes together, I thought about our wedding. Neither of us had much money, and I knew my parents wouldn't contribute much, if anything, so I imagined that we'd have a small wedding at our home, and Mom would cook. I wanted a house with a big backyard, not only for a garden but to host parties beyond our wedding.

When we found the place on Briar Ridge, Matthew and I both knew it was right. It was a 1200-square-foot, three-bedroom, two-bath home with a large deck in the back and lots of trees in the yard. It had big windows in the front, dark-painted walls, and a brick fireplace, and it was perfect for us. His mom and stepdad helped us move in on Valentine's Day.

That Christmas, we went to his mother's house. Everyone had opened their presents, but there was one tiny box left. Someone said, "Steph, I think that's for you." I picked it up and found a small ring inside. I was not expecting this. Not at this time, but I was very happy. I don't remember Matthew actually saying anything. We all just smiled and knew what the ring was for. I looked around the well-appointed house and the smiling family around me and realized this was about to be my family. It seemed like I had entered a completely different dimension, an alternate universe from where the family I grew up with resided. I wondered if this was the kind of home Matthew and I would create for our family...calm, safe, loving, and accepting. I said yes, and we all celebrated with champagne.

Beaming, I called Mom to tell her, and instead of saying congratulations, she told me what Hailey got for Christmas. I went back to the celebration a bit deflated but quickly recovered as we spread the news to other family members. We spent Christmas evening with Matthew's dad and stepmom, Lawrence and Debbie. They poured more champagne and made Matthew get down on one knee and officially propose. "Will you marry me?" he asked in the middle of the living room. I giggled and said yes, then we kissed and sat together, holding hands quietly on the couch while Debbie went back to making seafood gumbo. Matthew and I were not a couple that demanded attention or created fanfare and drama. We were quiet, predictable, and serene.

Planning our wedding on a shoestring budget, I started tapping my resources. Mom worked at a golf resort, and I asked if she could get us a free ballroom for the wedding. Better yet, she was able to get us a covered pavilion by a creek. Thanks to the contacts I'd made while networking, I knew a caterer who agreed to make our food and cake for just $500. Matthew's grandmother offered to pay for the flowers, and I found a brand-new wedding dress on eBay for $100. To top it all off, Lawrence and Debbie offered us their timeshare in Cabo, Mexico, for our honeymoon. Turns out, all my event-planning experience and connections made a beautiful wedding totally affordable.

The morning of our wedding, all my well-laid plans began to unravel. There was a tornado in Sun City, near the golf course, which made gathering under a pavilion a dangerous plan. I know rain is good luck, but getting carried away in a swirl of debris is not. But, if there's one thing I'm good at, it's quickly adapting to new situations. I didn't care if we got married in the cheap motel room Lacy had rented. I was getting married to a good man I loved.

The weather in Central Texas is a fickle thing and can transition through multiple seasons in a day. It might be balmy in the morning, hailing by late afternoon, and snowing by nightfall. Fortunately, this flip-flop weather worked in our favor, and the tornado that abruptly swept in and made a mess of things whisked away just as quickly. The rain stopped, the sky cleared, and everything was rearranged in time for our ceremony.

I had always been afraid Dad wouldn't be alive long enough to walk me down the aisle, and there he was with his hair pulled back in a ponytail, dressed in a suit and tie Mom had found at a local thrift store. It was the nicest I'd ever seen him, and he was looking at me with pride. He said, "Steph, you look beautiful. I'm proud of you. Matthew is a good man with a good family. You've done well." As he slowly walked me toward the altar, I reached for my mom's hand to walk with us too. It felt right for both of them to give me away, not just him.

I had never been a little girl who was always dreaming about her wedding day. I had so many other things on my mind as I grew up, but as I stood there on that perfect day, I realized why so many girls do. I looked around and saw 200 people who truly loved me...who had experienced extreme ups and downs with me, who believed in me even when I didn't, or who had loved and believed in Matthew. I looked into Matthew's eyes and could see tears of love and joy. I had no question in my mind that this man loved me. I was so incredibly grateful that we had found each other.

When it was over, Matthew and I drove my Honda Civic to our house and spent the night picking rice out of each other's hair while opening gifts and eating cake. One of the gifts we received was from Lacy. It was a box of matching dishes, a framed picture for our wall, and a pack of seeds. Lacy knew that all I ever wanted was a house with flowers in the yard, pictures on the walls, and matching dishes.

A few days later, we made our way to Cabo. Our room overlooked the wild blue ocean, and we spent a few calm days in paradise. We took a booze cruise to see the famous arc and ate dinner on the beach. We also went to the local market and made dinner for ourselves a few nights. When it was over, Matthew and I returned home relaxed and tan.

Leading up to the wedding, I had decided it was time for me to leave Shoreline — not because I didn't like it, but because I wanted to leave the restaurant industry. I felt limited there and wanted to explore my options. I was offered a job as a sales executive at 20/20 Payroll by a friend I had met through the Chamber of Commerce. Kendal was a dynamic and successful salesperson, and several members of her family had joined this young company. She and her husband, Mario, were charged with opening the Austin market, and they wanted me to be their first hire. Payroll seemed professional and like something that might lead me to other opportunities, so I accepted.

Unfortunately, the owner of 20/20 Payroll and the entire business was a complete fraud. We learned that he had been embezzling all the payroll funds we collected to fund his personal habits and toys. Though we were told not to rock the boat by attorneys and a representative from the FBI, I couldn't stand by as my clients continued to throw their money away and risk losing their businesses. I called or met with every single one of my clients and told them what had happened.

One of them was David Smith. I met him through networking while I was at Shoreline. He had a small but successful graphic design business, and he brought us on to do his payroll when he hired his first full-time employee. David worked out of his house, so I met him there with no makeup and my hair in a ponytail and cried the entire time while I told him what was happening and how to protect his business. He was quiet for a long time, and then he offered me a job. He said he wanted someone with that kind of integrity to work for him.

A sales position was not what I wanted at the time. I didn't want to put my face on another business, but I liked the idea of having an entry into an agency, so I told him that if I could learn everything about the business and work my way up, I would take it. He agreed, and I started selling graphic design for Envision Creative Group.

Working with Dave and Envision became a massive stepping-stone in my professional career. As we grew, we quickly realized that working from home was prohibitive for a design shop and employee morale, so we found an office downtown. It was a super cool loft on Fourth Street, above the gay bars. We felt like a real agency, and we were operating like one. We hired another designer, and I worked my way into an account management position while still bringing in the sales we needed. We even talked Dave into taking us on a trip to Mexico.

It started as a joke. We told him he could write the whole trip off if he took pictures and made a coffee-table book. He decided that we all deserved to get away, so he booked a small hotel that only had five rooms and paid for us and our spouses to go to Tulum, Mexico. The place was incredible. They had a party with bands, stilt walkers, and fire dancers on Saturday night, but the rest of the time, the place was pretty much ours. We explored Mayan ruins, went snorkeling, and ate delicious food. It was an amazing gift.

That wasn't the only free travel gift we received. Matthew had begun playing with The Doug Moreland Show, which was a popular Texas swing band. They traveled all over the state and always had an active audience. They were starting to book bigger and bigger shows and landed a week-long gig at the Texas Music Festival in Steamboat, Colorado. Since I was the band's number one fan, they gave me a pass and let me tag along, which was a blast. We'd ski all day, then drink beer and listen to Texas bands all night long. They were included in this festival for four years, and I was able to go every year.

The band was doing so well that they were asked to do a short tour in Europe. Four countries in fourteen days. I asked if I could go, and the band agreed. Included in the tour were all travel, lodging, and dining expenses. From the Netherlands to Germany to Belgium to France, it was a whirlwind tour of festivals and bar gigs, and we made the most of it. A lot of the gigs were in small towns, but while most of the band partied, a few of us took quick side excursions to places like Brussels and Neuschwanstein Castle. Though there wasn't much time for tourism, we got a good taste of the food, culture, and countryside. I could not believe this opportunity actually happened. It was absolutely heavenly. Lyon, France, was our last stop, up in the mountains outside of Paris. We finally had a chance to slow down, drink amazing wine, and enjoy the view. It was a perfectly romantic end to an otherwise hectic tour.

While whirlwind tours were fun, Matthew had been a full-time touring musician with Doug for a while, and he wasn't exactly a road guy. He liked to be home and have his personal space. He started thinking he should go back to school again, and after deep contemplation and conversation, we decided that a master's in psychology or therapy would be perfect for him. He already had many books on how the brain works, self-improvement, and other topics that aligned with these studies. With his background in education, he went to school to be a guidance counselor, but when he finished the program and was offered a job, it was snatched from him because he didn't have the proper length and breadth of teaching experience. With a few more classes, he graduated with a master's in counseling.

When Vicki's grandma passed away, Dad decided it was time to take care of her, so he and Mom moved into a trailer in Oklahoma. Mom was already complaining about how lazy Vicki was, so I didn't know how this would go. When Mom was young, she was sweet and fun, but as the years went by, she got angrier. I thought it was probably from living with Dad for so many years, but Dad blamed it on menopause and the aneurysm.

I picked Hailey up in Georgetown, and we drove up to spend Thanksgiving with the family and visit my grandma Rhodes. After dropping our things at Grandma's and visiting for a bit, Hailey and I went to hang out with Mom and Dad and catch up with Vicki. We were all drinking beers and having a good time when Dad said they were going to move back to Nevada. He said he missed the mountains and wanted to get back. I told him I didn't think that was a good idea. We went on talking about different things for a while, then he said, "Come here, baby, tell me why you don't think moving to Nevada is a good idea," and patted his lap. It wasn't a big deal for me to sit on his lap. I often sat on his or Mom's lap when they were drunk and happy. I put my arm around him, and I told him that Grandma was aging quickly and that Mom being there was a big help. I thought that Vicki should stay close to the town and the people she's known all her life, and that they have a lot of help there too.

Oops! That last part was the absolute worst thing to say. "Help? Who the fuck do you think helps us? You don't know what the fuck you're talking about. You're just a selfish fucking bitch who thinks she knows everything!" He stood up and kept yelling and screaming at me with his finger in my face. I grabbed my purse and told Hailey to get in the car. I could hear Mom yelling to stop fighting as I ran out of the house and

Dad followed. He was right behind me, and he hit the car window just as I closed the door. As I pulled away, Hailey looked at me and, with wide, tear-filled eyes, said, "He was going to hit you." I was thinking the same thing. I didn't see him again on that visit. In fact, I stopped talking to him altogether. I told Mom to call me because I wasn't going to call the house and accidentally catch him.

I thought avoiding my father was an obvious and easy fix until I started having panic attacks. They started in the middle of the night. I'd wake up feeling weird, and by the time I got to the bathroom, I'd lose all control, including my eyesight. I felt dizzy and like I had to vomit and defecate at the same time. It happened only a few times, and I didn't tell anyone. I thought it was random until I passed out during a photo shoot in Dallas. After that, Dave made me go to the doctor. I was certain I had a brain tumor, but she told me I just needed therapy.

With a little help from the therapist and Matthew, I learned how to keep Dad in my life with a few boundaries. Matthew had given me some tips before, but we could all see that it wasn't enough. I was so used to giving my all to everyone else while protecting myself physically that I had no idea how to protect myself emotionally. My therapist said that I could go through years of therapy to uncover all the trauma that was living within me, but she suggested I start by reading a book called *Adult Children of Alcoholics*. Though the stories were different from mine, the self-preservation tactics, the obsessive-compulsive habits, and the tendency to take care of everyone else before yourself hit deeply with me. Reading that book was like taking years of group therapy.

A few months later, I was in Las Vegas, celebrating my friend Beverly's fortieth birthday, when I received a call from Mom in the middle of the night. Dad had had several strokes and was in the hospital. On the verge of another panic attack, I paused to consider if I should go to him or not. I wanted to be there when he needed me and to say goodbye if I needed to, but I was also still holding onto a lifetime of anger and wasn't ready to test my new skills of emotional safety and boundaries until they were stronger.

The fear of losing him without saying goodbye won out over my self-protection, so I hopped on a plane and flew to Oklahoma. *Look who needs help now, Dad!* As one might imagine, my tough-as-nails dad pulled through. He was a little confused but still joked and flirted with the nurses, so we knew he'd be fine.

The only lasting impact was on his vision. Though he'd always been legally blind, his thick glasses got him through life until that point. The strokes, however, made it so he could only see outlines and shadows. Part of me was relieved, and part of me was ready to let go of him forever.

Chapter 18

When I was nearing thirty, I told Matthew that it wasn't imperative that we have kids, but if we did, he couldn't be a touring musician unless he was rich and famous and could pay for someone to help me. That wasn't an ultimatum. It was me understanding what it takes to raise a child. Matthew agreed with this, so I stopped taking birth control, and within a few months, I was pregnant. Matthew landed a job as a counselor, and everything was working according to plan.

I was so excited and eager to meet our baby and become a mama that I did what I always do and worked really hard at preparing for him to arrive. Covering all my bases, I did everything from yoga and Kegels to reading every magazine and book to eating as well as I could. I wanted to deliver naturally and for Matthew to be my coach. He was the calmest person I knew. We had at least four baby showers and received most of the things we needed and wanted. I turned our guest room into a nursery. We found out we were going to have a boy, and according to one of our baby books, I knew what size of fruit he was at every stage. Matthew made jokes throughout our classes, which made me think he wasn't taking things seriously. He didn't seem excited, but he was happy to feel our baby move from time to time, and he still made me feel beautiful even though I put on fifty pounds.

At Envision, we were quickly outgrowing our office, so Dave found a place in North Austin that was perfect. The only thing not perfect was that I couldn't help move or set up the new place. Dave and I had grown quite reliant on each other. He ran every decision past me and even talked of me running the business when it was time to retire. I loved that idea. I had always treated the business as if it was my own. For better or worse, everything was growing — the business, my belly, and a wariness that my parents were losing their ability to manage themselves or anyone else.

It became abundantly clear that it was not a good idea for my parents to move back to Nevada, but when had they ever let a bad idea hold them back? Vicki was not at all used to Dad's erratic behavior or to Mom's temper, and Mom was not equipped to handle Vicki. Vicki called the police almost every day or ran to the neighbors' houses begging for help. To make matters worse, Mom got arrested for driving under the influence. During her court appearance, she thought it was justifiable and appropriate to tell the judge that driving while drunk and high was a much better alternative than killing Vicki. No sympathy was provided. She got the ticket with all the fines and had to take anger management classes.

She must have borrowed money from Grandma because they moved back to Georgetown, Texas. A few days after they returned, Mom took Vicki to the gas station with her to buy a pack of cigarettes, and Vicki ran away. Vicki was lucky to knock on the door of a sweet woman who listened to her story. She then called Vicki's aunt in Claremore and told her everything. Within hours, she had all of Vicki's important prescriptions filled and purchased a new outfit and a plane ticket back to Oklahoma for her. We never spoke to or of Vicki again.

I started having contractions a few weeks before my due date, and my doctor said I would likely go into labor any day, but the date came and went without a baby. A week past my due date, we decided to try natural induction techniques. I was already experiencing so much pain that I truly thought my appendix had burst, but the doctors assured me that everything was fine; it was just the normal process and pains of labor. When we checked in, the nurse started to give me an IV so I could get an epidural. Apparently, there was nothing on my chart about a medication-free delivery, so the nurse took over and told me to start walking. After a few failed attempts to naturally induce labor, the doctor broke my water, and that was all I needed to move things along.

Matthew and I walked the halls and counted the minutes. Every time I had a contraction, he held me and calmly took me through my breathing. He stroked my hair and back and assured me I could do this. Only four hours later, I was giving the final push, and when I saw our sweet baby boy, I named him Liam Jackson Silver. He was perfect. Mom, Rosemary, and Michelle rushed in to meet him as soon as they could, but only after Matthew and I got some alone time with him. Matthew was so gentle and careful. He made sure that everyone was seated while holding him, everyone was sober, and that no one was wearing a shirt they had been smoking in.

We spent a few days in the hospital getting to know the ropes of being parents. I couldn't sleep at all. Between the beeps, the nurse visits, the feedings, and the anxiety I felt every time Liam left the room, I was a nervous wreck. Thank goodness Matthew was there with me. When we finally got home, the fear really hit me. Our dog Kelly ran out and jumped up, and I realized how scary it was to know I had to keep this precious baby alive and safe.

I had only four weeks of maternity leave, and while Matthew was home those first few weeks, he was truly helpful. We both changed every diaper and attended every cry together. I was shocked each time Liam wanted to eat again. Nursing hurt, and all I wanted to do was sleep, but I wanted to care for him the best I possibly could. No one, however, was taking care of me...including me.

Thanksgiving came just over a week after Liam was born, and because we didn't want to take Liam anywhere, I offered to host. I don't know what I was thinking! Matthew had to work that day, and Liam didn't want to be put down at all, so I started early in the morning and did one task at a time until everything was set and perfect. And then...I waited. Matthew was running late, and Mom and the gang hadn't even left their house in Georgetown yet. She was supposed to bring appetizers, and by the time they got there, everything I had prepared was cold. Although she denied it, Mom was high. I was sad, frustrated, and deeply exhausted.

The next few years solidified my recurring pattern of over-functioning and giving more than I had. I put everything I had into work and Liam. While Rosemary and Hardy moved to Austin for six months so that Liam didn't have to attend daycare so early, I still felt the weight of making sure we didn't take advantage of their generosity and time. Before Liam was born, I went to work early and stayed late. After he was born, I got there as late as I could and left as soon as I could. I didn't want to miss a moment with my baby. Liam woke up every two hours, sometimes four, even though he stopped nursing after four months. Matthew helped some, but he always asked for more sleep, and I always gave it to him. When I asked him to help, he didn't know what to do. After some intense arguing and pleas for help, he started vacuuming and doing a little laundry here and there, but it was clear to me that it was mostly my responsibility to take care of Liam. When I asked him about it...or when we fought about it, he told me he didn't have a mother's intuition; that he would play with him when he was old enough to play.

It's not fair to say that he did nothing. He loved Liam a lot, and he loved me too. He giggled and sang little songs, and he played the drums and juggled for him when he wasn't happy. I still couldn't help but think I was doing most of the childcare all on my own.

Though it was a lot more tiring than I expected, and my social life completely disappeared, I loved having Liam in my life. I took him for walks and to the park. We went to the grocery store every Saturday morning. He went everywhere with me when I wasn't at work. Watching him grow and change each day, learning all the foundations of life from lifting his head during tummy time to rolling himself over, was well worth the time and effort spent with him. He and I grew happier and closer with each new lesson learned.

Meanwhile, Envision was growing beyond anything we had expected. It wasn't easy by any means, but it seemed to be organic. Dave had promoted me to vice president, which meant I managed every client, every employee, and every contractor, and I helped with sales when we needed to close a big deal.

To say that I was stressed is an understatement, and Matthew and I didn't get much downtime, so Rosemary and Hardy took us on a short vacation to the coast. It was nice to be by the ocean, but being on vacation with a toddler isn't exactly being on vacation. It was nice to get away, I suppose, but I was just doing the same tasks in a prettier location — waking up at five o'clock in the morning, making meals, changing diapers, just with an ocean nearby.

To further sour the trip, Mom called and said that she and Dad had gotten into a fistfight, and she had a black eye. Things were really escalating between the two of them. After a big fight, Mom hit Dad in the head with an iron, so he took off to Oklahoma on a bus. Not wanting to live alone because Michelle and Hailey had moved in with another of Michelle's boyfriends, Mom decided to move to Oklahoma too. She was living with

Bobbie and his fiancé when she and Dad decided to meet up at a motel, and everything got nasty. What a mess.

After I hung up with Mom, Dave called in a panic about finances, and I had to assure him we had plenty of active projects and sales in the pipeline. It was not exactly the vacation of my dreams, but it was the best I could do at the moment.

Matthew and I knew we wanted two kids, and I thought I wanted them two years apart. When that time came, I wasn't quite ready, so we waited a few more months before I stopped taking birth control. This time I was pregnant within a month. I found a new doctor, and I knew the routine this time. Matthew would be my coach again because he was clearly gifted at it, and we didn't need any silly classes.

Again, I had a blessed pregnancy with no complications other than the fact that I started with twins but only had one baby. We lost the first one very early, so I kept my attention on the healthy one, which turned out to also be a boy. We named him Miles Joseph Silver, and he was also perfect. Liam was a bit disappointed he couldn't really play with his brother at first, but he was kind and gentle and tried to share his toys.

Rosemary and Hardy came back for the first four months, and she was so incredibly helpful again. Everything was a little easier since we knew what to expect, but it was still exhausting. Matthew and I were much calmer this time around, but I still didn't want to miss a minute with that little baby, and I was trying to be present for Liam too. Poor Matthew got the short end of the stick. He brought me coffee each morning as I nursed, not knowing I'd fallen asleep there during the night feeding. He put pillows and blankets in my car so I could nap at work, and he did what he knew to do to support me.

Rosemary and Hardy made friends with a couple in Austin who let them stay at their house so they could take care of Miles when he was an infant. The couple had a large property with a pool, and there was ample space between the houses in the neighborhood. After we visited a few times, Matthew told me he'd like to get a place like that — a place with distance between neighbors. I agreed but thought that was a pie-in-the-sky idea. Though I was doing well at Envision, I still didn't have a high salary, and Matthew was a counselor at a rehab center. We were far from poor, but finances were tight. I knew that our money needed to be used elsewhere.

He started looking anyway. At first, I was mad. I didn't want to take time to pack up the boys and go look at houses when we weren't actually going to buy one, and I couldn't imagine having to stage our house with all the toys and bottles everywhere. He told me I needed to dream big, though. He said if you don't dream, you don't go anywhere, and I knew that to be true.

Matthew worked his network, and he got a great job. Because of his master's degrees and teacher's certification, his salary would allow us a larger mortgage. He also asked Lawrence, his dad, if they would buy our house from us and rent it out. The market was good in Austin, and he could make a big profit.

One of our house-hunting adventures led us down a windy, two-lane road into the Hill Country to an area known as Driftwood. Only twenty minutes outside of Austin, the road to Driftwood felt like an instant switching of gears, from busy urban life to slow country living. Driftwood was magical. Open fields dotted with live oak trees lined the narrow winding roads. Wildflowers painted the ditches in the spring, and the air felt somehow thicker and sweeter out there. It was just what we needed.

When we pulled into a neighborhood, I thought there was no way we could afford anything, but when we stopped outside the house, my heart leaped. Could this really be ours one day soon? Across a huge front lawn was a perfect limestone ranch-style house. A winding driveway lined with 300-year-old oak trees led to a wide garage and, behind that, a forest. I was starting to dream big.

I strapped Miles to my back and took Liam by the hand, and we walked inside with the realtor. The house was decorated for Christmas, which made it look like something out of a holiday movie. The kitchen was larger than our current living room, and the pantry was almost as big as Miles' nursery. Floor-to-ceiling windows looked out onto an expansive lawn of green, where I was quick to imagine playing with the boys. The property was almost two acres, and half of it was wooded. Behind the property was a ranch. It was getting dark, and I didn't feel comfortable walking around outside with Liam and Miles, so Matthew explored the outside while I explored the inside.

The master bedroom was so large I could imagine our furniture looking like doll furniture, but when I saw the bathroom, I was in awe. There was a huge tub with a separate stand-up shower on one wall and a wrap-around counter with two sinks on the other wall. This bathroom was definitely larger than Miles' nursery, and the closet was enough to make most people drool.

I could tell Matthew was excited when we got back in the car. "Do you really think we can do it?" I asked. "We're going to try," he said.

Lawrence wanted us to have this perfect home, too, so he purchased Briar Ridge, and we put that money down on our new home in Driftwood. We had lived on Briar Ridge Drive for ten years, given birth to two amazing humans, and shared so many memories. It was strange to leave it behind.

Packing was a bitch, just like I thought it would be. I was the expert, and Matthew wasn't much help. Between wrangling kids, trying to juggle work, and packing up ten years of accumulated stuff, it was quite a job, but it was worth it. For the first time in my life, I hired movers, which was a game changer. I took one day off work on the day of the move. We met the movers at Briar Ridge and got them started, then met the truck at our new house in Driftwood. I immediately started unpacking as quickly as I could. The boys were at daycare, and that was going to be the only day my hands would be free. I made sure to set Liam's room up as close to his other room as possible so that he would feel at home, but he didn't really need it. When we brought him home to the new house that night, he ran around in circles, amazed at how huge this new house was.

While Rosemary was watching the boys, Matthew took me outside to explore the yard. He held my hand and showed me the porch swing that hung from an oak branch behind the fire pit and the trail that led to the back of the property. He pointed out every possible climbing tree, and we imagined the boys playing for hours in the woods. After we got the boys to sleep that night, I lay on the couch with Matthew, and he told me that even if we were only in this house for a year, it would be worth it. I agreed.

Matthew and I had accomplished a lot together, and even though I had hosted millionaires, movie stars, and politicians at Shoreline, helped grow an agency from the ground up, and put myself through college, I never quite felt like I was good enough until I moved into that house. For the first time in my life, when I met someone of high importance or walked into a nice house, I felt like an equal, like I didn't have to hide or pretend to be worth the time they were giving me. I know that worthiness is an inside job, and a house is just a thing, but for a girl who'd grown up the way I did, being dragged around so much that it looked like my parents were on the lam, this house meant something.

Matthew got a job at a location east of Austin, and I worked in North Austin, which meant that we each had at least a one-hour commute to work. Daycare was on my way, so I was in charge of pick-ups and drop-offs. Matthew usually left before I did and arrived home after. We moved to the country to slow things down, but everything during the work week was much faster. It was all we could do to coordinate our responsibilities in the city with a daily drive to the country.

A new neighbor moved in down the street and stopped by to introduce himself. He said his son was too old to use the playscape that was left behind, and he asked if we wanted it. Of course, we did. He left, and about an hour later, he and a friend rolled a huge playscape down the street to our house. Talk about a warm welcome to the neighborhood! It was the kind of playscape that had three swings, a playhouse on the top with a climbing wall leading up to it, and a tire swing beneath. The boys and I giggled with shock and excitement at the sight of this huge thing being wheeled into our perfect yard and under a perfect oak tree. They came back a little later and attached a slide. It was the addition we didn't know we needed to slow us down and entertain us on the weekends. We pushed hard through the weekdays so we could coast on weekends together.

Shortly before Thanksgiving, Mom called to say that Grandma Rhodes was taking a quick downturn, and they didn't think she had much time left. Mom went to Oklahoma to help, and Grandma died peacefully in her bedroom with all of her living children by her side. It was fitting that she passed only a few days before Thanksgiving, the one holiday for which our entire family continued to gather in Wagoner. Everyone congregated at her house, and we served all the things we did every year, but nothing tasted quite the same.

Chapter 19

Often, I thought about calling this book about my life *The Other Side of the Middle*. Not only had I finally made it to the middle class, but I'd landed all the way to the other side...and stayed there. No yo-yoing between a four-bedroom lake house and a homeless shelter, as I did with my parents. No more real struggle. I purchased all organic foods and didn't pay much attention to the price. We put Liam and Miles into private school. I bought clothes that fit well and more matching dishes and all the plants and flowers I could fit in my garden. We weren't rolling in dough by any means, but Matthew and I had each gotten small raises along the way, and we were comfortable, which was a feeling I'd craved my entire life.

At Envision, Dave treated me like a business partner. He took me to several conferences in New York, Boston, and California, and we were getting bigger and bigger clients. We landed a massive hotel account, which was our biggest client yet. They were planning to renovate their downtown Austin location and needed an agency to create branding for four new restaurants and launch them through internal and external marketing. This would have been easy for a larger agency, or if our contact had been helpful in putting together timelines and budgets, but neither one of those was true in this case. Like everything else, I assured everyone I had it covered, and I got to work. I did have it covered. I put together the strategy, timeline, and ad schedule. I managed all the creative aspects, from copywriting to design to print, and developed amazing press kits. I planned and executed a wedding giveaway for the new event venue and developed the in-house marketing materials. My contact at the hotel didn't even appreciate how much work we were doing or how little their budget was, but that didn't stop me from performing my best. I did all this while continuing to manage all the other clients, team members, and Envision as a whole...and I started having panic attacks again. This time I knew what they were, but they were just as scary.

Although my home life was going well, I felt like I was missing out on the most important years of my boys' lives. Five days a week, it was dinner, bath, and bed, and then waking up the next day to a mad rush of getting out of the house and doing it all over again. As I've learned, nothing lasts forever, but while I had a sense that some kind of change needed to be made, I wasn't aware of how much change was eventually in store for me.

We hosted Christmas at our house, and everyone came. Mom, Dad, Michelle, Bobbie and his girlfriend, Rosemary and Hardy, Lawrence and Debbie. It's rare that one can say this about such a robust family gathering, but the day was as flawless as a holiday can get. We started the morning with just the four of us, opening stockings and gifts, and then the crowd grew as I cooked dinner. I set up an extra table in the playroom and used all our Christmas and wedding china. The food was delicious, and everyone got along. When I sat in the playroom with Mom and our gang, she was surprised I chose to sit with her, but I told her I wanted to spend time with her. Mom beamed with joy in a way I'll never forget.

Life in Driftwood had really filled out with monthly potlucks and get-togethers with our neighbors and friends. The adults talked and laughed while all the kids played for hours in the yard. Most weeknights, the four of us sat around the dinner table talking about our day. It was almost like *Leave it to Beaver*, that is, if Beaver's mother was being a perfect homemaker while living a double life as a corporate executive.

I started to see that even though I was vice president, Dave wasn't going to make me a partner in the business, and I couldn't afford to buy half of it. I started to wonder what else I could do, but I didn't think I had any transferable skills. I wasn't a copywriter. I wasn't a designer. I wasn't a web developer. I wasn't a marketing strategist. I managed people. How do you put that on a resume? What job do I even go after if I don't want to be an account manager? I didn't want that level of stress anymore, but I wanted to keep the flexibility of seniority. I mean, I still only got a few weeks of paid vacation every year, which I mostly used when the boys were sick, but if I wanted to go on a field trip with the boys or if I needed an extra day because I actually got sick, I'd just take it.

I didn't get sick very often, or when I did, it was mostly when the boys were sick too, but I came down with a really bad case of the flu. It was a Saturday, so the boys were home, and we had a long-standing rule of little to no screen time. Matthew was working in the yard all day, so I entertained the boys, took lots of Advil, and counted the minutes until I could crawl back into my bed.

The universe had a different plan for me. As soon as I lay down, my mind started racing. I thought about work and how I would change it if it were my own business: what types of clients I would take, what services I would offer. The more I thought about it, the more excited I got. I stayed awake until about one o'clock in the morning and woke quickly the next morning. I typed everything up, and it still made sense.

I decided I would start my own business. A marketing and branding agency that served conscious companies and leaders. We'd coach them through their branding process, not just create an identity. We'd bring them on retreats to the Hill Country so that they could calm their minds and feed their souls and come up with more creative solutions for their business problems.

I was still sick and exhausted, and the boys were still home, but I was somehow energized as well. We played on the playscape for hours, and I wondered how I'd tell Dave.

That night I went to bed still feverish, both literally and figuratively. I was itching to get this started. Something in me told me this was the path to my dreams.

I stayed home on Monday, resting and gathering my thoughts, and at the end of the day, I decided to pitch it to Dave as a transition for Envision.

On Tuesday morning, I walked into the office, and everyone looked at me strangely. They said, "You're clearly sick, but you are also glowing, and you have an insane amount of energy. You are grinning from ear to ear and bouncing off the walls." Dave is the kind of person who doesn't like anything hanging in the air, so he pulled me into the boardroom to talk. I took out my notebook and laid out my plan. I told him it would be a great way to create a niche for ourselves and that the team would be so excited to get behind it. He took a deep breath, thought about it, and told me he understood that I was passionate about all those things, but it wasn't the right time, and probably not the right fit for Envision. We talked for a little while longer, and I walked out of the boardroom knowing that I was about to go out on my own.

When Matthew arrived home that night, I poured myself a glass of wine, looked at him, and told him I was going to start my own business. I was scared, but Matthew was more scared than I was. Shortly after, I gave a one-year notice to Dave. After fourteen years of working together, he was shocked and wanted me to stay, but he could see I had made up my mind, so he started looking for a new account manager. Dave hired the first account manager who applied. She was young and had no experience and would save him a little bit of money. I spent the next few months preparing for transition and training my replacement during the day, and planning my new venture after I put the boys to bed.

On Good Friday, I wanted to take the boys up to see Mom, but she said she wasn't feeling well. We hadn't seen her in a while, so I told her we'd just dye some eggs and let her rest. She hadn't been feeling well for some time, but she always drank a lot, so I assumed it was related to that.

When I went out to pack the car, I noticed that a hummingbird was stuck in our garage. We had very high ceilings for storage, so it would have had to drop down about ten feet in order to get out. It looked panicked and was flying erratically, and I tried everything I could to help it. At first, I grabbed a fishing net but then realized I'd end up falling and breaking my neck trying to save the bird. I pulled some flowerpots around to entice it down and left it alone while I got the boys and the rest of our things together. When we came out to check on the hummingbird, it was resting on a wall, so I thought that was a good time to leave and I'd help the bird when we returned.

When I got to Mom, she was still in bed. It was close to noon, and she had a wheelchair by her bed. She had complained about her leg hurting, but I didn't realize it was that bad. When I helped her into the chair, her body felt smaller than it had before; she'd been losing weight. Mom went outside to watch the boys and smoke a cigarette while I boiled eggs, and I asked Dad how long she had been that way. He said it had been a couple of weeks, and she was not doing well. We stayed for about an hour, dyeing the eggs, and then we left.

When we returned home, I walked out onto the deck, and our old cat Zoey gently placed a present on my foot. She had always been feisty, but she was not a hunter, and this was the first gift she had ever brought me in thirteen years. I looked down to see the dead hummingbird, and I instantly knew that my mother was going to die, and there was nothing I could do to control it. How I knew it was a sign, I can't say for sure, but it was as clear as if it were a memory and not foreshadowing.

The next day, we went out to the Foxes ranch to celebrate Easter like we always did. Over the years, we'd celebrated birthdays and holidays together as if they were my God-given family. In fact, they were. They were the biggest gift I had ever received. After the big egg hunt, I was flying kites with Miles and Liam when I received a call from Mom. She had spent the night in the emergency room, and no one was available to pick her up to take her home. No friends were reliable, responsible, or caring enough. I told Matthew I needed to go but that I'd be back. Diann asked if everything was okay. I held back the tears, took a deep breath, and somehow forced out a word. "No." I didn't have the strength to say anything else.

Mom met me at the front door of the ER, being pushed in a wheelchair by a nurse. He handed me some paperwork and told me the follow-up instructions and lab results were in there. I looked at it for a minute and quickly realized I had no idea what all those big words meant. I asked him what the results of the tests were, and he said he couldn't legally tell me, but it wasn't good, and I needed to make follow-up appointments as soon as possible.

Working was difficult when I knew I was on my way out and Mom was very sick. Even though I had gotten the sign and I also knew in my heart something big was happening to her, I still had to try. I made the appointments and took her to several doctors, one of whom was an oncologist. He didn't like that Mom had lost so much weight so quickly, and he asked her all sorts of questions about drugs and habits. In full Mom fashion, she made jokes along the way. "Do you take pills?" "Why, you got any?" Mom's jokes made me giggle but also frustrated me as I could see the behavior of the doctor change from concern to frustration. When he asked if Mom had a history of cancer in her family, she said no. *But wait, I thought that my Uncle Justin and Grandma Rhodes both died from cancer.* She didn't seem to remember that. I couldn't tell if she was high or losing it. The oncologist told us we needed to see a gastroenterologist, so I made the next appointment and took her.

The physician's assistant for the gastroenterologist walked into the room with kind concern on her face. She told me I needed to take Mom to an oncologist as soon as possible. I told her that's who sent us to her, and I saw her face become frustrated and calmly angry. She looked me in the eyes, then looked at Mom and asked if he had told us what the test results from the emergency room visit revealed. No, he hadn't. She said that Mom had cancer all through her abdomen. It had fully taken over her liver, which meant it would quickly spread throughout her body, if it hadn't already. She was strong and kind, but I could tell she was upset when she told me I needed to spend as much time with my mom as I could. She gave me some numbers to call to find help with pain medication because she had a feeling the oncologist wouldn't be very helpful; then, she stood up and gave Mom a hug. She put her hand on my shoulder and looked me in the eyes before quietly walking out of the room.

When we got in the car, Mom asked what had just happened. She wanted to know what we would do next. I looked into her eyes and said, "Mom, you have cancer." Then we drove silently back to her apartment. When we arrived, Dad was sitting outside smoking a cigarette, and Mom walked right past him without saying a word. I sat down beside him. He said, "Well?" while he was looking at the ground. I quietly told him the diagnosis, and all he said was, "Shit. Okay."

I walked into Mom's room, and she was silently sobbing. I wrapped my arms and my body around her and cried with her. She told me she didn't want to die. She said she knew she had cancer months ago. Not because anyone told her but because she could feel it. "I'm so sorry. I'm so sorry. I love you." That's all I could say.

Eventually, I got up and drove to the drugstore to pick up her medication. I was numb, but I knew I needed to make calls again. I called Michelle first. She asked if she needed to come now or if she should wait. "I think you need to be here," I said. She went back and forth, thinking Mom would need more help if things got worse, and I told her that there is no way to know when things may get worse but that if it were me, I'd come now. The next call was to Aunt Marilyn, my mom's sister and closest friend. She was upset and asked a lot of questions I couldn't answer, but I told her she needed to come too.

I paced through Walgreens and called Bobbie next. I knew he didn't have much money, but I told him we'd cover gas and food if he could make the trip.

After hugging my mom again, I went home and squeezed my boys more tightly than ever before. I fell into Matthew's arms and told him that I needed his help. I didn't know how long it would be, but I'd be sleeping at Mom's every other night so that I could make sure she was eating and felt loved.

Mom went back to the emergency room a few days later. Her pain was too great. Michelle arrived just in time to give me a little break. She stayed with Mom every day. They ran some more tests, and we waited for the results. The same oncologist we had seen before confirmed that Mom had cancer throughout her body, including in her brain.

I climbed into the hospital bed with Mom, wrapped my arms around her again, and told her that I loved her. "I know, baby girl. I love you too," she said.

Mom grew tired of being in the hospital and didn't think the nurses were keeping up with her main meds enough, even though they were giving her fentanyl. She told us that all she wanted to do was go home, smoke some cigarettes, look at her flowers, and talk to her neighbors. That's exactly what we did. She was so weak that she couldn't hold her cigarette without dropping it, so we put a towel over her lap to keep her from burning herself. She noticed that her roses were about to bloom and asked me to keep watering her other plants. Mom was a terrible gardener, but she loved plants and flowers and always had a bunch of plants that were half-dead. I told her I'd take care of them, and she went to bed.

Bobbie and Aunt Marilyn arrived the next day, and we took Mom back to the oncologist to see what her options were. Mom had no strength, and even though she had lost weight, she was still probably 200 pounds. We wheeled her to the van and hoisted her in, then carried her into the doctor's office. He suggested she get fluids while we talked. Getting her to the fluid chair was a lot more difficult than any of us expected. She fell in the middle of the floor and had no strength to assist us in getting back up.

The doctor gave us all sorts of options, including hospice. Marilyn took notes the whole time so that she could report to the rest of the family in Oklahoma, but when we got home, it was clear to me that hospice was the only option. Mom was already losing her ability to speak and had no control over her body. To put her through treatment would be torture for everyone. We all agreed.

One month of hell. That's what it felt like. I drove from home hospice in Georgetown to work, to Driftwood, to work, and back again, falling asleep with my boys in my arms every other night, and alternately staying up all night nursing my mom and wondering if each moment would be her last. In the midst of caring for my mom, I took calls from Dave, who was panicking about different members of our core team leaving Envision. I had a full plate of sales calls and meetings, and I put together proposals and kept up with my emails. Working hard, pushing forward is what I knew how to do.

My aunts and uncle brought a travel trailer and sat by Mom's side for a few days. Mom had completely lost her ability to talk, but they prayed for her and told her they loved her. Dad was respectful and appreciative of them, but the same couldn't be said for some of the other family members. He told Michelle and Bobbie's aunt Nancy to get the fuck out of his house, and he picked a fistfight with Greg, Michelle's boyfriend. The fistfight led to Mom being moved in the middle of the night to an assisted living facility.

Earlier that day, Dad had gone into the room to talk to Mom for the first time. He started to tell her that he was going to be okay. He had a plan. Mom had been gazing out the window, but she turned her head toward him and mustered up the strength and courage to say, "Get out." It came as a whisper, but it was clear. I was in the back of the room, and Dad looked at me quizzically. "Dad," I said softly, "I think she told you to get out. You need to leave the room." Mom had dedicated most of her adult life to following this man back and forth across the country. She'd taken care of him when he was sick, and put up with all the names and words that would have made a military man cry, and now, in her time of need and pain, he continued to think and talk about his own needs. She was finally done taking care of him.

Michelle, Bobbie, Aunt Marilyn, and I took shifts with Mom, never leaving her alone. One night, Bobbie and I stayed together, and as Mom and Bobbie slept, I could hear her gargle and struggle to breathe. I begged the nurses for help, but there was nothing they could do, so I curled up into a ball on a chair and cried, feeling smaller than a field mouse.

The next morning, I called Michelle and told her everyone needed to be there today because this was going to be her last day. Then I went into the hallway and had a Zoom sales call.

Everyone arrived, and we all told Mom we loved her; we stroked her hair, and we told her it was okay. Then she turned her head to the window and let out her last breath.

After crying and hugging for a while, we decided we needed to tell Dad. I texted Matthew to tell him she was gone, and Aunt Marilyn stayed in the room so that Mom still wouldn't be left alone. Dad had no interest in going to say goodbye. He hadn't seen her since she was wheeled away on a gurney the night of the fight, and he thought she wanted it that way.

I clipped a white rose that had bloomed from Mom's garden, and we went back to the room. Matthew was standing with Mom's body. I didn't expect him to be there. I had never expected anyone to show up for me unless I asked them to, but there he was. I placed the rose on her chest and fell into him again, shaking and sobbing.

Michelle and I signed the papers for Mom's body to be cremated, and I asked them to keep the rose with her. I didn't have the bad visions I did when she had her aneurysm. This time I knew it was her time. We had a small wake at the bowling alley where she worked. I didn't tell anyone about it. I didn't have the strength. Matthew and the boys were there. Bobbie and Michelle were there. That's all I needed.

I finished up my work with Envision, making a few big mistakes that pushed me out earlier than I had planned. I tried my best to do everything right but was juggling way too many things at once.

When I left Envision, a few clients followed me. One of them I cleared with Dave, and the other I didn't. I actually tried to talk the client into staying, but he said his relationship over the years had been with me, and he didn't like working with the new account manager or designer they put him with. It was his decision, but I avoided the difficult conversation with Dave.

I started working from home, where I could focus on serving the few clients I had. To keep myself from overworking or getting too stressed out, I started having mandatory dance breaks. I also donated marketing efforts and time to the boys' school to help the PTA with fundraising.

No more before-care or aftercare for my boys! I calmly took them to school in the mornings and picked them up right at three every afternoon. We played so much, and I was the driver for every field trip. Liam was six and Miles was four, and I was finally spending time with them the way I always wanted to.

Without Mom around, Dad was an absolute mess. Because of his strokes, he was legally blind and had no business living by himself. He should have gone to an assisted living home, but apparently, they don't allow chain-smoking and drinking handles of vodka, so I used HEB online to have groceries delivered to him weekly, and I visited him every month to clean the apartment (yuck) and visit for a bit. I was angry with him, though. I was mad that he didn't die first and that he never said goodbye to Mom. I understood that their relationship was complicated, but that wasn't a good enough excuse. She put up with his shit and took care of him for thirty-six years, and she loved him.

Dad also had trouble with his throat. He survived polio as a kid and had difficulty swallowing, which was also exasperated by years of smoking and drinking. He often coughed so hard he'd cough up blood. The neighbor kids, who Mom used to feed and love on, started checking up on him and spending time with him. It was a bit ironic that the kids were half black because Dad had been a racist all his life. But he couldn't see, and he needed support.

In the middle of the night, eight months after Mom died, an ambulance was called to Dad's house because the kids next door heard pounding on the walls. Dad was taken to the hospital.

I went to visit and found a frail and failing father. He wanted coffee, but they wouldn't give him any because he would choke. After chatting for a little bit, Dad lifted his fist to his mouth, sipped the air, and said, "Mmmm, that's good coffee." I laughed at first, thinking he was making a joke, but he continued to hold the imaginary mug in his hand and sip it from time to time as he looked with awe out in front of him. Then he looked at me with pure love and said, "I love you, babe." I told him I loved him, too, and gave him a big hug. After I let go, he spread his arms wide open and said, "Look at this place; it's beautiful. We should buy it." I realized then that he was hallucinating. I'd never seen him so innocent and happy, so I went along with it. It became clear that he thought I was his first wife. In his mind, he was nineteen and in love. We talked about our home and our future for about an hour, and it was a side of my dad I didn't think he had. He showed me a time when he was proud and optimistic, and he unknowingly gave me a gift.

The hospice nurse sat with me, and we agreed that he wasn't going to last much longer. The only medication he was on was for his blood pressure, so we stopped that and focused on making him comfortable. I spent my nights at home with the boys, and my days sitting next to Dad. I worked some, but not like I had earlier in the year when Mom was dying. John and Diann Fox came to visit, and Michelle came back.

Within a week, Dad was gone. He left the earth when we were out to breakfast just after Bobbie arrived in town. Unlike Mom, he must have wanted to go alone.

I never realized just how alone Dad was until the three of us tried to plan a service. For Mom, her family came to say goodbye, along with her friends and coworkers and neighbors. But for Dad, it was just us and John and Diann. We put some photos on the TV stand and played Buddy Holly and other music from the '50s. His sister Lisa wanted nothing to do with him, and his brother didn't know him. In fact, when I called to break the news to his brother, we had a two-hour conversation, and it was the first conversation I'd ever had with him.

Dad was cremated too, and I spread both of their ashes in the gardens at the house. Actually, we saved some of Mom's ashes. Michelle, Bobbie, and I each got a little decorative box to put them in. Mine was in the garden, I held onto Bobbie's, and Michelle took hers.

I've never been afraid of death. Ever since I was about twenty, I've known that I'd already lived a lot of life. At each turn, I think that if I die now, I'm okay. I just don't want it to be super painful. I know that birth and death are painful. There's no way to get around that. We are literally moving from one universe to another, and that can't be painless, but if it can be minimized, I'd like that. The only way to minimize it is with love. To love and be loved, and to know you've lived life fully.

With both my parents on the other side of the veil, being on the other side of the middle means something different to me. I'd seen up-close what matters most, like good health and spending time with loving friends and family. Yes, it is lovely not to worry about how I'm going to pay the bills or about my children's safety, but the momentum it took to catapult me away from my trajectory of poverty took a toll. I didn't want to end up like my parents, constantly struggling and scraping by, but I also wasn't interested in a life of constant striving for external rewards. Instead, I wanted to thoughtfully and intentionally select who I included in my life, how I spent my time, and what I created. I suppose what I truly wanted was something in the middle.

Chapter 20

I've never been religious, except for that semester I lived with Grandma, but watching my parents die opened me up to a new type of spirituality. Sure, I had studied world religions in college because I wanted to know what the people of the world believe happens not just on the other side but here. Like, how does God talk to us? Are things actually pre-ordained? Are there spirits, ghosts, angels, and daemons that affect our daily lives? Christianity, Buddhism, Hinduism, Taoism, science, and everything in between offered both overlapping and conflicting answers. I'd always believed in ghosts and didn't give much thought to spirits and angels, but a new awareness of something much greater than all that was growing inside me. If hummingbirds could carry important messages, what else was possible?

Surprisingly, the summer that followed the trauma of my parents' deaths became one of the most joy-filled summers of my life. I had kids from all over the neighborhood running into my house for snacks and drinks as they rode bikes, played in the yard, and swam at each other's pools. I took Miles and Liam on adventures to all the creeks and swimming holes we'd missed out on while I had to work.

My business was growing organically with the few clients that came with me from Envision, those that were sent to me by referral, and a few that found me online. I had built a team of contractors I loved and trusted, and we were proud of the work we were producing.

Lawrence and Debbie came to town and took us all to dinner. They had always taken us to fancy restaurants, but this time seemed special, and it was. Matthew told me that one of his cousins worked for Tony Robbins, and he was able to get me a free ticket to Unleash the Power Within in New Jersey. He even spoke with an aunt who had an apartment in Manhattan and was going to let me stay with her. The entire trip was paid for; all I had to do was book the plane tickets. I went, and it was inspiring, exhausting, and addicting. I wanted to grow in all the ways possible. This was such a generous gift from Matthew, and one that put me on a trajectory of growth and healing.

I loved that I was spending more time with my family, but it became clear to me that too much of my time and energy was still going into work and stressful things, so I hired a coach. Matthew thought I'd pick one of the Tony Robbins guys, but I knew I didn't need a "Massive Change, Massive Action" guru. I needed someone who had a better understanding of the balances of life. Serendipitously, I was introduced to Bill Small. He was a musician and the father of one of Liam's classmates. After a quick chat, I learned that he'd been a coach for decades and believed in quantum physics. This was my guy...and his first assignment for me was to take time for myself. When I laughed, he told me he was serious and that he'd check in on me. It took me about a month to complete the assignment, but I did it.

Matthew started playing in bands again and was happy with work, but he told me that he'd felt like he either needed to go to group therapy or join Toastmasters. He couldn't quite put his finger on what he needed, but Toastmasters was the direction he chose. He found a great group in Dripping Springs that he could swing over to on Tuesdays after work. Even though he was an introvert, he thrived in Toastmasters. He'd come home on Tuesday nights just about the time I was reading bedtime stories to the boys and show us the ribbons he'd won each night. We all became close with a small segment of the group and started having dinner and pool parties. A few of them had kids the same ages as ours, so it was perfect.

I talked with Bill about starting a podcast, and he put me to work overcoming the fear. I landed the founder of Torchy's Tacos as my first guest and talked a videographer and a tradeshow guy into giving me products and services for trade to have a live interview at an Austin location. It was a smaller crowd than I'd hoped for, but the room was full enough to look like the real deal.

I was getting busy, and I started to feel lonely. Matthew worked until eight o'clock on Mondays, had Toastmasters until eight o'clock on Tuesdays and would sometimes hang out with the crowd after, and then he had rehearsals on this day or that day and gigs on Fridays and Saturdays. I loved having so much time with the boys, but I told Matthew I wanted him to want to be with me more. His answer was to put something on the calendar so he didn't book a gig. He didn't get it. I wanted him to WANT to be with me, to spend time with me.

And then came Covid. The next thing we knew, we were locked down, and locked in. No more parties, no more gigs, and no more school! Suddenly, like everyone, we had nothing but time together, along with lots of fear, anxiety, and uncertainty.

Immediately, I went into triage mode with clients, helping them try to find ways to pivot so their businesses could survive. Everything Matthew had been doing — work, music, and Toastmasters was canceled, and we feared he'd lose his job. With big bills to pay and financial uncertainty, we talked about the possibility of moving in with one of his parents or the Foxes if we needed to. I lost a few clients, reduced a few retainers, and held onto a few accounts, but my focus really became the kids since they couldn't play with friends. We were never so happy to have our big yard to play in. We climbed trees, rode bikes, and went for lots of walks. The three of us also had Fortnight dance parties and competitions, which was my absolute favorite.

The formerly live podcast moved to Zoom, which was a lifesaver. It was a lot of work to shift gears, but having deep conversations with professionals was my extrovert IV. Luckily, Matthew's employers realized that counseling was even more important than ever, so they set up online sessions, and Matthew turned his drum studio (our third bedroom) into his office.

I started having Zoom happy hours with friends and also decided that drinking alone wasn't too bad after all.

As soon as the bars opened up, Matthew wanted to go to a gig. In my mind, bars were the worst place to be. Schools still hadn't decided if they were going to open, but I let him make the decision, and he went.

With both of us home most of the time, Matthew and I finally had plenty of time to talk. We talked for hours and hours, in so many circles. We both agreed that we were unhappy enough to talk about not being together but not so unhappy to leave. I wasn't having panic attacks this time; I was in a constant state of panic, and so was Matthew. He came down with a case of shingles, and I got on anti-anxiety meds and drank too much. I even started smoking again and found myself sneaking out to the woods for a drink and a smoke, begging the universe for an answer to why I was so miserable and what to do about it. It was an incredibly tough year. We worked out, did yoga, meditated, played with the kids, made bread, gardened, and still kept coming back to the same circles of conversations.

The next summer was strange. Our home was heavy. We weren't in lockdown, but we didn't have the same flow of kids riding bikes and asking for snacks. Everything had changed. Matthew and I each got our own therapists and then decided marriage counseling would be good. We were truthful, honest, and genuine, but we still couldn't make it feel right. We both admitted that this would be easier if the other was overtly abusive. At least then, one of us would have a solid reason to leave. We'd have something to tell people that they would understand. Turns out few people are satisfied with a shrug and half-hearted, "Things just weren't working out anymore."

I finally decided that we weren't getting anywhere, and that we needed to get divorced. We'd been having so many open conversations I thought that we could plan everything out together and determine who gets what before meeting with attorneys, but I had something big I needed to do first.

I had always thought that when Mom and Dad died, we'd have a party, a celebration of life in Virginia City. Once Covid travel restrictions were lifted, I asked Michelle if she would go with me on Mom's birthday to spread her ashes and celebrate her. We wanted Bobbie to go with us, but he couldn't afford it. My Aunt Marylin and Beverly were able to go, though, and so were our cousins Crystal and Tamara.

On September 1, we all flew into Reno. Michelle, Tamara, and I all got tattoos to commemorate the event. I designed what I call "a charm bracelet of strength." Mine is around my ankle, and Michelle got the same one on her forearm. There are symbols of the moon, a female, an arrow, and a few other bits that symbolize growth and strength. After getting freshly inked, we drove up the mountain to VC the next day. It was eerie but nice. California was on fire, so the valley was filled with smoke, but the air was crisp. The small billboards leading into town were exactly the same as I remembered, and almost nothing about the town had changed. A few stores were different, but all of my parents' regular haunts stood just as precariously as they had decades earlier when I ran to tell Mom that Bobbie had broken his arm.

As we checked into the same motel where Michelle and I met Colt and Cody, Aunt Marylin pulled out the Solo cups and filled them to the brim with vodka and Squirt. I called Justin, who worked with me at Calamity Jane's, and he met us out at a restaurant. We spent the rest of the night drinking at The Mark Twain and planning our adventure for the next day.

It was Mom's birthday, September 3. After breakfast, we poured ourselves some drinks, and Justin drove us around town. At each location where we lived, Michelle and I said a little statement, clinked our cups, and sprinkled a bit of Mom's ashes. We lived in at least nine places in this tiny little town, with the apartments above Red's counting as three. When we were done, we decided to do tourist things, like walking on the same boardwalks Michelle and I did as children.

I was so incredibly happy that night. I felt like we were in exactly the right place at the right time. I was talking to a couple we met, and the man looked at me and slowly said, "You are so beautiful!" His girlfriend nodded her head and agreed. Someone had told me the same thing earlier in the day, so I went to the bathroom to see what was so different. My hair was a little nicer because I didn't have to fight Texas humidity, but everything else looked about the same. In fact, we'd consumed quite a bit of vodka over the past few days, so I knew I didn't look rested, but then it hit me...I looked happy. My light was shining so brightly that others could see its beauty and just couldn't quite put their finger on it.

The next day, we shopped in the shops, had lunch at Red's Candies, and prepared to go home. I walked through town with confidence, power, and joy — far different than I felt any of the times I had lived there before. I remembered to call Matthew but spent most of the call telling him about the spiritual connections that had been surfacing for me. I knew he'd think I was crazy, but I was learning to get comfortable just being myself.

Two weeks later, I had one more bit of travel before I could concentrate on what the rest of my life was going to look like. I had been helping a friend start a fintech company. Like a lot of startups, he had recruited several people to work for free in hopes of big payouts when it all took off. I'd donated all the branding and a lot of my time, and he was going to Las Vegas for a pitch jam in front of several investors. I went with him to help seal a deal and to meet up with my friends Christina from St. George and Virginia from Mesquite.

The visit with friends was great, but we didn't come home with any checks. Instead, Matthew informed me that he had filed for divorce while I was gone. Alright, I guess it was time to talk about how we were going to split everything. What were we going to do with the house and, most importantly, the kids? I thought we could negotiate and figure everything out together, but every time I asked him what he thought about a certain idea, he would say, "That's an interesting idea. I'll talk with my attorney about it." At first, I thought he was just too overwhelmed, but then I realized his attorney had advised him not to negotiate anything with me. Our time for talking was over.

I knew that the best thing for the boys was for me to keep the house and have primary custody. After all, this was the only home they really remembered, and I was their primary caregiver. I always had been. I also knew, however, that I was their true home and that anywhere I ended up, they would feel comfortable and loved. Matthew had made it clear that he wanted to keep the house, so I knew it wouldn't be an easy fight to keep it, and I wasn't sure if I could afford to keep it, even with child support. We'd saved up some cash and had some investments, but I didn't know how much of that would end up going to attorneys. We also had a house full of quality furniture to think about. It was all too much, so I continued to sneak out to the woods, but instead of sneaking a smoke or a drink, I decided to seek advice from God and the universe.

I took a few crystals out with some tarot cards. I figured if I couldn't find the answers on my own, perhaps I could conjure them from beyond. I took citrine for strength, green fluorite for the heart, and amethyst for universal wisdom. I took a deep breath and asked for guidance, then drew a card in front of each stone. I was knocked off my feet that each card aligned with the intention of the stone. I didn't know the cards well enough to read them by the image alone. I had a book I referenced, and together, the message was clear.

You have been through too much not to think you have the strength to move through this challenge. You are filled with great love, and those around you know that. No change in space or possessions will change your love. Wherever you go, you will make a home.

So that was it. My questions were answered clearly, and I knew that I could leave the house behind. I'd been guided, this time without a dead bird as my messenger.

I fought for primary custody of Liam and Miles, and I relinquished the house and all the furniture in it as a gift for Matthew and the boys to have as a stable place to always come back to. At the same time, I gave the boys and me an opportunity for a new adventure. Our now ancient cat, Zoey, came with us.

I knew I could do this because I had done it so many times before — start a new life, in a new house, with new dreams. It would be tough, but in my bones, I knew that I had the strength to build a home wherever I went. This time, I had a network of friends and colleagues I could take with me and two amazing, loving boys to keep me going.

Just ten years earlier, no amount of convincing would have made me believe that after finally checking off the boxes of marriage, a big career, and a spacious house in the country that I would have not just the desire but also the strength to un-check them all. I'd worked for and gotten everything I'd ever wanted, which was far more than I could have ever imagined as a kid, only to give most of it back. And yet, I gained more by letting go than I expected.

It was in leaping into the unknown that I pieced together a new version of my life that was less paint-by-numbers and more improvisation — an inspired and artful collection of parts that were chosen with intention. My business has bloomed to include more offerings like coaching, retreats, and wellness experiences. My connection with Spirit has grown from hiding in the woods with my tarot cards to a daily practice that infuses and informs all aspects of my life. And the days the kids are at my house, they get a version of me that is real and present and totally engaged.

Of course, it hasn't been all easy. I miss my boys every second they aren't with me, my relationship with the in-laws has completely changed, and managing finances for a home on my own is tougher than I imagined. I often think about Matthew and wonder if there was something we could have done differently to keep things together. But the lessons I learned from my childhood have provided me with strength and resilience and an ease of knowing that there really is no bottom to hit, and no top to reach. I'm limited only by my thoughts and dreams.

For a time, my external trophies were important. They gave me confidence and a sense of belonging in places I might not have dared to tread. But, in truth, the only thing I ever need to keep going, to keep creating, and to keep loving, is the light I already carry inside me. No angry parent, or demanding client, or divorce, or lost job, or broken ankle, or missed opportunity can take away the good that's always meant for me.

The light will always find a way to shine if I let it.

I will always let it.

THE END

AND ANOTHER BEGINNING

Acknowledgments

Because this is a memoir, the thanks are not just about the accomplishments of the completion of these pages; they are about and to those who helped me get from "there to here."

Mom and Dad were wild and unpredictable. They taught me about life and having a willingness to live it. I do not agree with the decisions they made. In fact, I've intentionally made many of my own life decisions in direct opposition to theirs, but I greatly appreciate the love and free spirit they instilled in me. Because of their willingness to leave everything behind time and again, I understand that nothing is permanent and nothing is more important than the ones you love. Mom and Dad also taught me the value of hard work and a job well done. Unfortunately, I didn't realize until after I lost them both just how proud they were of me and how much Mom quietly admired and cheered for me.

Michelle and Bobbie are literally the loves of my life. They are my roots and my wings. Thank you both for your belief in me, for your trust in me, and for letting your life be seen alongside mine.

Thank you to Lacy and Rachel for being my first and best remember-when friends. You know all of me, and still love me.

Matthew. Thank you for loving me, believing in me, teaching me the power of boundaries, showing me the world, growing with me, and giving me the gift of our two amazing children.

My two amazing children - Thank you for being silly, serious, and everything in between. You changed my life in every way, and I love every moment with each of you.

Beverly - we chatted in line for breakfast at a networking function, and you've been my best supporter and cheerleader ever since. I know you'll never tell where all the bodies are buried, and neither will I. Thank you for always believing in me and being on Team Steph.

Jeffrey Weinberger left us a few years ago, but he provided an eager young waitress with an opportunity, and that was my bridge...the beginning of the path to my dreams.

David Smith saw honesty and integrity in me...perhaps also a cute butt, but that's not how I got the job. I sat next to you for fourteen years, and you trusted me with your entire business. You taught me more than I ever imagined I even needed to know, and you became one of my absolute best friends and cheerleaders. Most of all, you helped me see my strength and my worth when I didn't.

The Fox Family is the greatest gift I have ever received. God knew that I needed a safe, stable, dependable, sweet, and fun family that I could always count on. John and Diann - I cannot thank you enough for choosing me. Jared, Chris, and Sam - you may not have grown up with a sister, but we will grow old together.

Thank you to Michelle Savage for not thinking I was too crazy when I called from a cell phone talking about starting this project as a podcast and had to let you go because I accidentally let a horse loose on the road. I knew when I met you that you were going to be the one who helped me make this story come to life.

Bill Small has helped me see that who I am is calm, inspired, and full of love - not frantic, small, and full of fear. Thank you for helping me to see that I don't need to work like a dog or blow shit up to feel comfortable.

So many people have stepped in as parents and guides for me along the way. My aunts and uncles, Rosalie and Homer, parents of friends, Rosemary and Debbie, and of course, Sherie, whose last name I'm not sure I ever knew. Thank you for trusting me when others didn't, for seeing something in me worth helping or saving, and for attaching a parachute when I leapt without looking.

Lastly, I'd like to acknowledge all the artists, musicians, and writers who expanded my world and opened me up to who I could become. I discovered this poem in my second year of college and thought of it as the thing that gave me the courage to move to Austin. I printed and framed it, and I've kept it visible for many years as a reminder to keep leaping. When I read it now, I realize that it has been in my bones since birth. I hope it does something for you too.

W. H. Auden's "Leap Before You Look"

The sense of danger must not disappear:
The way is certainly both short and steep,
However gradual it looks from here;
Look if you like, but you will have to leap.

Tough-minded men get mushy in their sleep
And break the by-laws any fool can keep;
It is not the convention but the fear

That has a tendency to disappear.

The worried efforts of the busy heap,
The dirt, the imprecision, and the beer
Produce a few smart wisecracks every year;
Laugh if you can, but you will have to leap.

The clothes that are considered right to wear
Will not be either sensible or cheap,
So long as we consent to live like sheep
And never mention those who disappear.

Much can be said for social savoir-faire,
But to rejoice when no one else is there
Is even harder than it is to weep;
No one is watching, but you have to leap.

A solitude ten thousand fathoms deep
Sustains the bed on which we lie, my dear:
Although I love you, you will have to leap;
Our dream of safety has to disappear.